*The Texas Republic
and the Mormon Kingdom of God*

"LIEUTENANT-GENERAL" JOSEPH SMITH REVIEWING THE NAUVOO LEGION.

NUMBER TWO
South Texas Regional Studies
Sponsored by Texas A&M-Kingsville
Ward B. Albro, General Editor

The Texas Republic
and the
Mormon Kingdom of God

MICHAEL SCOTT VAN WAGENEN

Texas A&M University Press
College Station

LIBRARY OF CONGRESS CATALOGING-IN-PUBLICATION DATA

Van Wagenen, Michael.
The Texas Republic and the Mormon kingdom of God /
Michael Scott Van Wagenen.— 1st ed.
p. cm. — (South Texas regional studies ; no. 2)
Includes bibliographical references and index.
ISBN 1-58544-184-8 (cloth : alk. paper)
1. Mormon pioneers—Texas—History—19th century. 2. Frontier and pioneer
life—Texas. 3. Smith, Joseph, 1805–1844. 4. Houston, Sam, 1793–1863—Relations
with Mormons. 5. Texas—History—Republic, 1836–1846. 6. Texas—History—
1846–1950. 7. Mormons—Texas—History—19th century.
I. Title. II. Series.
F395.M8 V36   2002
976.4'04—dc21
2001006772

*For
Monica
Maya
and
Brodie*

Contents

CONTENTS

Illustrations

Maps

Preface

I first became aware of Mormon settlements in Texas while I myself was a Mormon missionary in the Texas hill country. My missionary training did not include any history lessons, so, during my first assignment in Kerrville, when I heard whisperings of an ill-fated Mormon experiment, I was more than a little surprised. In fact, during my two years of missionary service, several towns that played important roles in this story—Austin, Zodiac, Fredericksburg, and Bandera—all came under my ecclesiastical jurisdiction at one time or another. At the time I had no appreciation of these stories, nor did many people living in these towns. It seemed that the Mormon settlements were nothing more than rumor, even among Mormons themselves.

I would not know of the significance of these places in my own religious history if it were not for reading Fawn M. Brodie's *No Man Knows My History*. In this controversial work Brodie mentions Joseph Smith's attempt to purchase parts of Texas for use as a Mormon homeland. That immediately brought the stories of Texas Mormons back into my memory and sent me on the search that has ultimately culminated in the writing of this book.

Several historians have written on the Mormon colonial movement in Texas over the years. They have brought to light many important documents, and I am indebted to their pioneering efforts. This study varies from previously written works in that it focuses on the negotiations of 1844 rather than the resulting colonies. In addition the study of Mormons in Texas has often lacked a Texas Republic perspective. I hope that by adding this side of the story, I have created a well-rounded work that will prove valuable to Mormon and Texan historians alike.

Also significant is that I wrote this book in Port Isabel, Texas, a town that would have been crucial to the proposed Mormon nation. It would have served as a principal port for the Mormons, providing an essential link to Mexican, Texan, and U.S. trade. Port Isabel would have also been an obvious port of entry for the thousands of Mormon emigrants from Europe who flooded in during the mid-nineteenth century.

If one is prone to speculation, the social, political, and cultural implications for this area are staggering. Nevertheless history is not about speculation—it is based in reality. Yet, more than 150 years later, reality is hard to determine, as some key facts remain hidden, lost, or forgotten. The Church of Jesus Christ of Latter-day Saints has the answers to many mysteries raised by this study, but it chooses to keep official records of the Texas negotiations private. That is their prerogative. The state of Texas likewise might have had some answers. Unfortunately documentation of the negotiations has disappeared, if it ever existed at all. This leaves a fragmentary record of official documents.

Luckily many participants in the Texas-Mormon experience kept journals or wrote memoirs. These writings helped in piecing together the crucial events of the spring of 1844. In addition, the Republic of Texas and the Church of Jesus Christ of Latter-day Saints both kept detailed records during this time. Although I did not have access to all materials, the great majority of existing records have been made available to me. Perhaps at some future date the church will release additional documents to the academic community. When that happens, a new chapter in this story can be written.

Acknowledgments

During my research many historians helped me: D. Michael Quinn, William Slaughter, Ronald Romig, Melvin C. Johnson, Robert Flanders, Lola Van Wagenen, Leonard J. Arrington, Davis Bitton, Martha Bradley, Klaus Hansen, and others. Also helpful was Elbert Peck at the Sunstone Foundation. I am grateful for the time these people shared with me.

I must also thank Juliet V. Garcia, James Sullivan, Manuel Medrano, and Mimosa Stephenson at the University of Texas at Brownsville and Texas Southmost College for their guidance, thoughtful comments, and willingness to help. In addition I am grateful to James Seymour for acting as my unpaid editor and encouraging me to always consider the Gentile perspective.

I owe a tremendous debt of gratitude to my wife, Monica Delgado, for her constant help and support through this process, and to my daughter, Maya, who spent her first months of life buried in the library with me. I also thank my extended family for their unfailing support.

Last, I would like to thank Antonio N. Zavaleta, at the University of Texas at Brownsville and Texas Southmost College. In addition to making my graduate education possible, he opened doors, found scholarships, arranged employment, and served as my mentor throughout this interesting process.

I dedicate this work to the memory of Dr. Leonard Arrington, who remains an inspiration to all Mormon historians, and to Phillip Sumsion, a fellow missionary in southern Texas who died too young.

The Texas Republic
and the Mormon Kingdom of God

Introduction

From its earliest days of colonization, Texas sparked the imagination and ambition of some of North America's greatest leaders. Joseph Smith, Jr., the founder of the Church of Jesus Christ of Latter-day Saints, was one such person. After several unsuccessful attempts at creating a separate society within the borders of the United States, Smith began to look for other alternatives.

The year was 1844, and Smith was living in Nauvoo, a virtual city-state on the Illinois bank of the Mississippi River. With more than fifteen thousand residents, Nauvoo was the masterwork of the young prophet's life. In spite of his successes, Smith knew his days in Nauvoo were numbered. Political jealousies raged in nearby communities. Unpopular religious teachings including polygamy, Christian socialism, and the use of scripture other than the Bible raised the ire of religionists throughout the nation. Perhaps most significant, Smith's blending of church and state, known as the "Kingdom of God," deeply offended the sensibilities of most Americans. With his power weakening in Illinois and armed mobs at his gates, Smith looked outside the borders of the United States for both refuge and empire.

During this time Smith closely followed the challenges and victories of the Texas Republic through Nauvoo's secular and religious newspapers. The Texas Republic intrigued Smith, and he came up with three solutions to his domestic problems, all involving the Republic. First he nominated himself for president of the United States on a platform of Texas annexation. Then he appealed to Congress for permission to raise a volunteer army to guard the Texas and Oregon frontiers. If these first two options failed, Smith could negotiate with Sam Houston to purchase the sparsely populated and highly contested southern and western regions of the Texas Republic. There Smith planned to establish a theocratic nation that would serve as a buffer between Texas and Mexico. In this Mormon Kingdom of God, Smith and his followers would be free to practice their religious beliefs without interference from the United States. Smith appointed an ambassador to the Texas Republic, and secret negotiations began in earnest.

These were also desperate times for Texas president Sam Houston. His predecessor had provoked the wrath of the Comanches on the western frontier, and Antonio López de Santa Anna was amassing troops on the disputed southern border. To make matters worse, the U.S. Congress was balking on the annexation issue. He was desperate, in debt, and looking for assistance from England, France, or perhaps even the Mormons.

It is worthwhile to explore the unusual political environment found in the borderlands at the time, involving the personalities of Houston and Smith and the common ground on which the Texas-Mormon relationship was based. Also fruitful is the examination of the aftermath of the ill-fated plan. In spite of apparent failures, there is a lasting legacy to be found in the Texas-Mormon experience. Smith sent one colonizing party into the Republic. These people were a part of early Texas history and eventually blended into the greater Texas culture. Houston remained sympathetic to the Mormon cause as a U.S. congressman. He was a critic of the Utah War in 1857 and helped bring an end to that conflict.

The Church of Jesus Christ of Latter-day Saints also changed as a result of this process. Houston's advocacy eventually helped the United States to accept the church. As Mormons found a place within the United States, they abandoned their desire to form a political "Kingdom of God" and eventually assimilated into mainstream American culture. Ultimately Texas and the Church of Jesus Christ of Latter-day Saints played significant parts in each other's development and destiny.

CHAPTER I

The Emergence of Nations in the Southwest

The first half of the nineteenth century saw the unprecedented rise of independent nations around the world. The fire of independence and anticolonialism sparked by the American and French revolutions flared across the oceans to the far reaches of the globe. Leaders, selected by natural talents rather than by birthright, began to wrestle the reins of power from decrepit monarchs and colonial masters.

By far the most impressive nation building in the world was in the Americas. Mexico, Guatemala, El Salvador, Nicaragua, Honduras, Costa Rica, the Dominican Republic, Venezuela, Colombia, Ecuador, Peru, Bolivia, Paraguay, Chile, Argentina, Uruguay, and Brazil all gained independence between the years 1811 and 1841.

It is little wonder that reports of nation building around the hemisphere inspired the creative minds of natural leaders in the American Southwest. Both Americans and Mexicans saw opportunities to carve out nations from unsettled territories in Mexico, the United States, or the lands disputed by the two countries. The short-lived nations that emerged in the American Southwest during this era included the Republic of Fredonia (1826–27), the Texas Republic (1836–46), the Republic of the Rio Grande (1840), the California Republic (1846), and the State of Deseret (1849–51). The legality of each of these would-be nations was questionable, resulting in challenges from both the United States and Mexico. Mexico sent troops to the rebellious northern frontier and subsequently defeated the Republic of Fredonia and the Republic of the Rio Grande. The Texas Republic and California Republic, on the other hand, defended themselves against Mexico until they were annexed by the United States.

The land claimed by the State of Deseret was annexed by the United States at the end of the U.S.–Mexican War in 1848. It was later occupied by the U.S. Army in 1858 to enforce federal control of the region.

A lesser-known nation was also planned in the American Southwest in 1844. Cryptically called the Kingdom of God, this theocratic state was the result of negotiations between President Houston of the Texas Republic and Joseph Smith, Jr., the founder of the Church of Jesus Christ of Latter-day Saints.[1] The proposed state would have been located in the territory between the Rio Grande and the Nueces River, land claimed by both Mexico and the Texas Republic at the time. Had the plan been a success, it would have greatly altered the history, culture, and settlement patterns of the American West and Southwest.

Although the plan was eventually abandoned, the events surrounding the proposal of this theocratic nation in the Texas-Mexico borderlands are important to a broader understanding of the history of both Texas and the Church of Jesus Christ of Latter-day Saints. These events provide further insight into the adversity and unusual political climate that existed in the American frontier during the mid nineteenth century. The events show the lengths Houston and Smith were willing to go to achieve the twin goals of security and self-rule for their people.

On December 20, 1841, Houston gave the first speech of several that he was to give to the Texas Congress during his second term as Texas president. In this speech he explained the three main challenges to Texas security. The first was the weak Texas economy. Second was warfare with the Native Americans on the western border. The third, and perhaps most pressing problem for the young republic, remained its hostile relations with Mexico. Houston vowed to resolve these issues as quickly as possible.[2]

On the very day Houston gave his speech, Smith, far to the north of the Texas Republic, wrote a proclamation to his people about their involvement in state politics.[3] Mob violence and regional warfare had forced his fledgling religion, the Church of Jesus Christ of Latter-day Saints, from homes in New York, Ohio, and Missouri. Now, in an obscure corner of Illinois, he hoped to make a fresh start. Smith's lack of influence in state government always worked to his disadvantage. His unorthodox style of Christianity often provoked the wrath of his neighbors. Without a voice in the government, he was powerless to protect his own people. In 1838, for example, Gov. Lilburn Boggs of Missouri issued an order of extermination against the members of the church, or Mormons, as they were commonly called.[4] In Nauvoo, Illinois, along the banks of the Mississippi River, Smith planned to flex the political muscle of his church.

Whether or not Houston and Smith realized it at the time, both had the potential to solve each other's problems. Smith was looking for a place where he could govern supremely—a land where he would be free to practice his religion without interference from the outside. He had financial assets, a theology inherently sympathetic toward Native Americans, and, above all, a large army. Houston, on the other hand, had millions of acres of land to sell or give away. Unlike territory in the United States, this land was outside the control of the enemies of the church. It was land where a people could theoretically start a nation and live life according to their own will and conscience. In 1841 the time was not yet right, as both Houston and Smith were pursuing other options to solve their problems. The failure of these options over the following years would bring the interests of these men together in a way that no one could have expected.

To fully understand the circumstances that brought Texas and the Mormons to the bargaining table, it is first necessary to understand the background of both the Texas Republic and the Mormon religion in America.[5] Both Houston and Smith's identities and personalities were intertwined with the movements they represented. Both men committed themselves unquestioningly to their respective causes.

Houston first came to Texas in 1832, at the age of thirty-nine.[6] He was a war hero, a former governor of Tennessee, a former ambassador of the Cherokee Nation, and a man looking for a fresh start.[7] Texas provided that in those days. Beginning with Mexico's independence in 1821, American and European citizens began relocating to the Texas frontier. The Mexican government made generous concessions if the foreign colonists would embrace Roman Catholicism and swear allegiance to Mexico. For several years the system seemed to work, until Mexico's conservative Centralist Party began restricting the rights of the country's citizens. Allies of the Federalist form of government, established by the Mexican Constitution of 1824, began fighting back in isolated regional rebellions. Texans largely supported the Federalists, and in 1835 a full-fledged revolution erupted in Texas.[8]

Sam Houston, 1844. *Courtesy The University of Texas
Institute of Texan Cultures, No. 72-3511*

From the beginning Houston positioned himself in the middle of the
Texas conflict. His experience in the military and in government back in
Tennessee made him a natural leader. After several bloody battles and
many casualties on both sides, Houston's forces captured Mexican president Antonio López de Santa Anna at the Battle of San Jacinto. Under
duress Santa Anna signed the Treaties of Velasco, establishing the
Republic of Texas as an independent nation.[9] This defeat haunted the
Mexican president for the rest of his life and inspired him to make
numerous attempts to reclaim Texas.[10]

Although Texans were creators of an independent republic, most
desired annexation by the United States.[11] The northern United States
feared that the annexation of Texas would spread slavery throughout the

Southwest and tip the political balance of power toward the southern states.[12] The northern states' resistance to annexation postponed any decisive action by the United States for several years.[13] As a result Texas remained an independent nation. With that autonomy came great financial, political, and military responsibility and also instability. In the first elections of the Texas Republic, Houston became president.[14] He immediately set about trying to stabilize the economy, make treaties with the Native Americans on his western frontier, and defend his border with Mexico.

Houston's greatest problem with Mexico throughout the Republic period was the disputed southern and western boundaries between the nations. At the negotiating table, following his capture at San Jacinto, Santa Anna made a secret agreement with Houston that established the boundary of Texas at the Rio Grande. Once safely back in Mexico, Santa Anna refused to acknowledge the boundary agreement and claimed the traditional Texas border lay at the Nueces River. This created a disputed territory between the Nueces River and the Rio Grande that was called the Nueces Strip.[15]

Although the inhospitable land of the Nueces Strip was defensible enough, the lack of Anglo settlers in the area made the region a nightmare for the Texas Republic.[16] Throughout the period of the Republic, Anglo control of the land never extended south of Refugio or west of Castroville.[17] A few outposts were established beyond this area, but they remained small and did not attract settlers during this time.[18] During his first term as president, Houston sought peace with both the Comanches and Mexico. Through his restraint Houston managed some semblance of peace with Native Americans and maintained the border with Mexico.

According to the Texas Constitution, a president was not allowed two terms in a row. As a result Mirabeau Lamar was elected to the office of president of the Republic in 1837.[19] During Lamar's presidency the Republic's economy floundered as the government churned out devalued paper money.[20] Lamar's intolerant policies toward the Native Americans provoked the wrath of the Comanches, who repeatedly raided settlements in the Republic.[21] Finally his hawkish attitude toward Mexico weakened any chance of a peaceful resolution of the border dispute. Mexican troops crossed the Rio Bravo with impunity as Santa Anna amassed troops along the river throughout Lamar's presidency.[22] Had it not been for internal disorder in Mexico, Santa Anna might have launched a full-scale invasion as early as 1837.[23]

Aware of its precarious situation in 1840, the Texas government supported the formation of the Republic of the Rio Grande to serve as a buffer between Texas and Mexico. This short-lived nation straddled both sides of the southern Rio Grande and included both citizens of Texas and Mexico who supported the Mexican Constitution of 1824. More important to the Texas Republic, the Republic of the Rio Grande created the illusion of a barrier between the belligerent nations. In spite of the help of Texas volunteers, Mexican troops soon reconquered the territory south of the Rio Bravo, leaving the Nueces Strip once again undefended.[24]

When Houston took office again in December, 1841, he headed a nation weakened by currency devaluation and war. President Santa Anna perceived the vulnerable condition of the Republic. As rebellion subsided at home, he ordered a series of military campaigns to harass Texas. The first of these came just days after Houston began his second term. In a surprise move Gen. Rafael Vásquez, commanding five hundred men, crossed the Rio Bravo and captured the city of San Antonio.[25] The Mexican army made several other successful incursions into Texas over the next twelve months, taking a heavy toll on Texas morale and depleting resources. In 1843 an armistice signed between Mexico and Texas led to an uneasy truce along the Rio Bravo.[26]

Houston quickly realized that he needed to populate the unoccupied lands with friendly colonists in order to defend the territorial claims of Texas. This was the same logic that the Mexican government had followed in allowing the foreign colonization of Texas in 1821 under the *empresario* system. Just like the early Mexican federalists, Houston offered broad concessions of land to any group of colonists willing to settle in the unoccupied regions of the Republic.[27]

From the framing of the Texas Constitution there were plans to promote immigration to the Republic. Initially these plans targeted individuals or even families.[28] Then in December, 1840, the Franco-Texienne Bill reached the floor of the Texas Congress. This bill proposed to grant three million acres to a group of eight thousand French colonists and soldiers. The bill also offered the French additional concessions related to mineral rights and taxes. The bill was controversial and was narrowly defeated. The main opposition to the bill was that it gave a foreign nation too much control in Texas.[29]

On February 4, 1841, the Texas Congress passed another bill that addressed the colonizing program in Texas. "An Act Granting Land to Emigrants" was a less radical plan that deeded certain territory and privileges to a group known as the Peters Colony.[30] The Texas Congress gave further concessions to the colonists with the sole requirement that they settle in the unpopulated lands of the Republic. Just weeks after Houston began his second term as president, he broadened the law to include all potential colonists.[31]

The Texas government began an aggressive campaign to attract American, English, and French settlers to its frontier. There was a natural tendency in the Republic to favor emigrants from the United States. Americans, however, were generally too individualistic to participate in any colonization program. Americans also wanted to settle in the safest and best lands in eastern Texas. Foreigners, primarily French and German, were financially desperate and would not question their land grants in the southern and western parts of the Republic. As a result President Houston and Congress settled foreigners on the less-desirable frontier lands where they were a buffer against further attacks from Mexico or Native Americans.[32]

Houston gave several land grants west of San Antonio and south of Refugio. He even offered a large land grant in the disputed Nueces Strip to a group of French colonists. Unfortunately for Houston the French colonial agents could not recruit the needed settlers. In spite of the generous offer of land, most Europeans could not be enticed to settle in these dangerous areas, and the Texas *empresario* system did not populate the frontier. Regardless of optimistic projections only a handful of permanent towns were settled. The Texas Congress eventually revoked most of the colonial charters since the colonial agents did not attract enough immigrants to make the program viable.[33]

Apparently the failure of the Texas colonial movement was one factor encouraging the 1842 military incursions from Mexico.[34] Antonio López de Santa Anna remained confident that Anglo settlers could not create the buffer zone in the south that Houston so desperately needed. So long as Texas remained without military allies, her claims of nationhood would be challenged. It must have been frustrating for Houston to hear reports of Mexican soldiers marching unopposed through the Nueces Strip. Had the French colonists settled that land, perhaps they could have provided some line of defense.

In 1843 President Houston negotiated an uneasy truce with Mexico. As the expiration of the truce neared and with annexation to the United States still an elusive dream, Houston began to entertain more radical options. The time was right for any group of colonists willing to bring a large population of settlers to Texas.

In this environment the Mormons, with their assets in the United States, their tolerant attitude toward Native Americans, and their own means of defense, made overtures to the Republic of Texas. By 1844 they had a church membership of approximately twenty thousand people, valuable property holdings in Illinois, and, perhaps most important, a professionally trained militia of more than five thousand men.[35] Like the Texans, the Mormons were a people forged in adversity, and they were not averse to taking up arms in their own defense. Many Mormons had lost family and friends to the ravages and violence of frontier life. Outcasts in their own country, their history and rise to prominence closely paralleled the time frame of the Texas Republic.

CHAPTER 2

Joseph Smith and the Mormons, 1830–44

In 1820, a year before the first Anglo settlers began immigrating to Texas, a fourteen-year-old New York farm boy named Joseph Smith, Jr., began to have a series of visions. Smith claimed that Jesus Christ had told him that true Christianity had vanished from the earth because of the gradual corruption of the early Christian church. Smith further claimed that Jesus had chosen him to be a prophet with a mission to restore the true Church of Christ back to the earth. Key to this restoration was the translation of a book of scripture known as the Book of Mormon.[1]

Smith published his new book of scripture in 1830 and distributed it throughout New England. He soon convinced a growing number of followers of the validity of the Book of Mormon. On April 6, 1830, Smith organized a church, initially called the Church of Christ, in Fayette Township, New York.[2]

Within weeks Smith organized a missionary force and sent them through the countryside in search of converts. Inherent within Mormonism was the gathering of the membership into communities. Similar to many utopian and millennial groups of the time, this arrangement not only reinforced homogeneity, but also provided some protection against the religious intolerance found in frontier America. In a short time tens and then hundreds began to gather with the "Saints," as the Mormons preferred to call themselves.

In the early months of the church, a Mormon missionary named Parley P. Pratt stopped in the quiet town of Kirtland, Ohio, to proselytize the local townspeople.[3] Kirtland was a Campbellite community built under the inspiration of Christian communalist and millenarian

Alexander Campbell.[4] Many within that faith believed firmly that they would soon receive signs and direction regarding the second coming of Christ and the subsequent thousand-year millennium of peace. Pratt found fertile ground among the Campbellites for the new Mormon gospel. As a result several hundred Campbellites joined the Mormons, including the spiritual leader of the community, Sidney Rigdon. Within months Kirtland converted from being a Campbellite community to being a Mormon community.[5]

Smith's claim of visions and his use of the Book of Mormon in conjunction with the Bible immediately caused problems in New York. Local ministers were particularly vocal against the Mormons and had Smith arrested for preaching from the Book of Mormon.[6] In December, 1830, as problems increased with non-Mormon neighbors, Smith claimed that a revelation from God had ordered him to move his New York congregation to Kirtland, Ohio.[7] A small group of Mormons then moved beyond Ohio and began settling in Missouri in order to preach to Native Americans in the Delaware tribe.[8]

In July, 1831, Smith reported another revelation in which God had told him to establish a gathering place for the church in Missouri.[9] Smith then commanded several hundred followers to move to just outside Independence, Missouri, to establish a city called Zion.[10] In Zion the Mormons would create a new society and prepare for the second coming of Jesus Christ. For the next seven years the Mormons would maintain communities in both Ohio and Missouri.

Membership in the church was quickly growing. Young families living on the frontier seemed most drawn to the church. Within two years the church had grown from six members to more than two thousand. By 1840 the Mormons numbered more than five thousand.[11] The increasing population began to worry the once-tolerant neighbors of the Mormons. Students of both Mormon and U.S. history are often surprised at the unusual amount of persecution perpetrated against the Mormons during the nineteenth century. Some of the largest mob actions in United States history were committed against them.[12] In the years between 1830 and 1846, thousands of Mormons were driven from their homes under the threat of death. There has been much speculation as to exactly why the Mormons drew such violent reprisals in the nineteenth century. A few reasons are worth exploring for a fuller understanding of why the Mormons would seek to leave the United States.[13]

The most obvious reason for Mormon persecution was the church's unorthodox theology. In creating his new religion Smith integrated elements of Native American belief, Jewish mysticism, Freemasonry, Egyptology, and New England folk magic with Protestant Christianity.[14] This unusual theological mix had surprising appeal in the early days of the church. Protestant ministers competing for converts in the West felt threatened by the thousands who were converting to Mormonism. Mormons widely believed, and certainly there was proof, that mainstream ministers were often the instigators of the persecutions they suffered.[15]

The next cause of Mormon persecution dealt with the sheer numbers that were joining the religion. Many who had previously settled in Ohio, Missouri, and somewhat later in Illinois feared that the Mormons would outnumber them and hence take control of local or even state politics. People who tolerated the Mormons in small numbers suddenly turned violent when their counties filled with the Latter-day Saints. Many older residents resented Mormon economic competition. Working communally, Mormons thrived even in areas that earlier settlers had found undesirable. Also Mormons tended to support their own businesses to the exclusion of Gentile businesses.[16]

The economic success of the Mormons appealed to the basest motivation for persecution—greed. If the mobs could vilify the Mormons, then they could justify the plundering of Mormon possessions. Taken a step further, if the mobs could drive the Mormons out of the region, they could purchase Mormon homes and farms for little money or even take possession with no expenditure at all. As a result the Mormons lost millions of dollars' worth of property during their first sixteen years of existence. Much of this property fell into the hands of their enemies.[17]

Mormons, often viewed as conspirators, espoused the emancipation of African slaves and the assimilation of Native Americans into Euro-American society.[18] Because of these beliefs, highly exaggerated stories circulated about Mormon–Native American–African American military alliances. In Missouri these rumors caused considerable alarm since the slavery issue alone was enough to incite armed violence. From the church's earliest days Smith sent missionaries to several Native American tribes.

The Mormon belief that Native Americans were a part of God's chosen people contradicted the national policy of "Indian removal" then in practice in the United States. As the Mormons continued to preach among the Native American tribes of the West, they naturally attracted suspicion among the Gentile communities.[19]

Another reason for persecution was the structure of Mormon society itself. Although Mormonism was a uniquely American phenomena, outsiders often viewed it as inherently anti-American. Rather than espousing the rugged individualism valued in mainstream frontier culture, Mormons adopted clannish and community-oriented lifestyles. Smith refused to promote a passive, ritualistic, Sunday religion. Mormonism taught an entirely new way of life. Mormons in the 1830s practiced a kind of Christian communalism known as the United Order.[20] A general feeling prevailed among the neighbors of the Latter-day Saints that the Mormons must be of a lower character and class to live in such a way.[21]

The last reason for hatred of the church came from the Mormons' attempts to protect their own from prosecution. Smith and several church leaders had been jailed months at a time on false charges. Frequent manipulation of the law by the church's enemies obviated any protection it might have offered the Mormons. Judges and juries often acted as aggressive participants in the mob violence committed against the church. As a result a code of silence bound the Saints and thus revealed a growing contempt for the laws of the land. Lawbreakers, both in and out of the church, used this to their advantage. Although clearly exaggerated, stories circulated that Mormon communities provided havens for thieves and murderers.[22]

In 1833, shortly after Houston entered Texas, a group of freed slaves joined the Mormon faith and attempted to move into Missouri. The freedmen were foiled by a state law requiring proof of citizenship. When a Mormon newspaper printed the statute, Missourians assumed that Mormons were helping free African Americans to skirt the law. Tempers flared and soon mobs were converging on the Saints in Jackson County.[23]

In Independence a Gentile mob of five hundred armed men organized and drew up a proclamation that demanded the immediate removal of all five thousand Mormons from the county.[24] Given only fifteen minutes to comply, the Mormons refused to leave their homes. Over the next several weeks mobs burned dozens of houses and physically assaulted several church members. Afraid that the Mormons might fight back, the governor ordered all weapons belonging to Mormons confiscated. Without any means of defense and with mob attacks getting bolder, the Saints were forced from their city of Zion north into Caldwell County. They quickly organized themselves in two new communities, called Far West and Diahmen.[25]

Smith still remained in Ohio when the mobs drove the Saints from Jackson County. When he received word of the attacks, he was outraged. Prior to this assault, the Mormons had been peaceful people, even in the midst of persecution. The indignation Smith felt that day forever changed his pacific attitude. He quickly organized the first of two militia groups that would eventually serve under him. He named his small group of two hundred volunteers Zion's Camp and began the nearly one-thousand-mile march to Jackson County.

The presence of Zion's Camp in Missouri only made things worse for the Mormons. Although the militia was meant to protect the unarmed brethren, inaccurate rumors spread across the countryside that Zion's Camp was coming to lay waste to the state. As a result thousands of Missouri militiamen gathered spontaneously for the defense of the state. Mormons in Caldwell County were kidnaped and held as hostages. With only two hundred men Smith was greatly outnumbered. His first experience in leading an army was a failure, and he was forced to back down and lead his weary troops back into Ohio.[26]

For a few years the Mormons maintained a relatively quiet but strained peace in both Ohio and northern Missouri. By 1838 the once-amicable relations between Mormons and Gentiles in Ohio had completely disintegrated. Jealousies, false rumors, and a growing religious intolerance brought mob violence to the doors of the once-peaceful Kirtland community. As the Kirtland Saints fled to Missouri, the situation there also worsened. An angry mob, fearing that Mormons were tipping the scales in local politics, barred Mormons from the ballot box in Gallatin. The Mormons resisted and fighting broke out. The violence at the ballots led to an armed skirmish between Mormons and their neighbors at Crooked

River.[27] Reports reached Gov. Lilburn Boggs that the Mormons were in open rebellion. The governor was notorious for his contempt for Mormons and was looking for an excuse to deal harshly with them. On October 27, 1838, Governor Boggs issued the following proclamation to the state militia, which sealed the fate of the Latter-day Saints in Missouri: "Your orders are to hasten your operations and endeavor to reach Richmond, in Ray County, with all possible speed. The Mormons must be treated as enemies and must be exterminated or driven from the state, if necessary for the public good. Their outrages are beyond all description."[28]

Encouraged by the legal justifications of their actions, the mobs became bolder and more violent in their attacks. Hundreds of homes were burned in the fall and winter of 1838. Smith gathered the church membership together in the town of Far West and prepared to meet a force of six thousand state militia. After he received word that thirty-two Mormon settlers working in a nearby milling community had been brutally shot, he was devastated. He had no stomach for further bloodshed and surrendered himself to the Missouri state militia in an attempt to stop further violence against his people.[29]

A kangaroo court made up of Missouri militia leaders condemned Smith and other church leaders to death for treason. As they were being prepared for the firing squad, a compassionate militia general named Alexander Doniphan argued against the legality of the punishment and barely prevented their execution.[30] Smith was instead jailed pending a state trial. The general populace of the church received no mercy from the militia and was soon driven from Missouri into Illinois. Missouri authorities incarcerated Smith and several other church leaders in the town of Liberty as they awaited trial. While in prison, the Mormon leaders suffered torture and other forms of inhumane treatment, including being fed the flesh of a murdered slave. In April, 1839, after six months of imprisonment, a sympathetic sheriff allowed the Mormons to escape during a prison transfer. With the general Mormon population out of the state, the calls for Smith's life temporarily subsided.[31]

Later that month Smith and his fellow prisoners caught up with five thousand Mormon exiles on the Illinois bank of the Mississippi River. There Smith purchased a village named Commerce, renamed it Nauvoo, and began his life's greatest work. Immediately the Saints set to work on building a new home. Initially fellow residents of Hancock County admired the industriousness of the Latter-day Saints. Within a year a large city rose from what had once been a swamp.[32]

In spite of apparent successes in Illinois, the Mormons still suffered from their financial losses in Missouri. Mormon attempts to win reparations in Missouri courts proved futile. In February, 1840, Smith made an appeal to the federal government in Washington, D.C., for assistance. He first made a visit to President Martin Van Buren. Van Buren was so caught up in the sectional politics of the time that he told Smith and his cohorts, "Gentlemen, your cause is just, but I can do nothing for you. If I take up for you I shall lose the vote of Missouri." Smith then turned to Congress. Smith had a frustrating interview with state's rights advocate Sen. John C. Calhoun, who also had no interest in interfering with Missouri affairs. The dejected prophet realized his case was hopeless and left Washington in disgust.[33]

Smith now knew he could not rely on the federal government for aid or protection. To avoid the same mistreatment meted out in Missouri, Smith realized he had to win broad concessions from the Illinois state legislature in Springfield. In early 1840, a distinguished visitor, Dr. John C. Bennett, called on Smith in Nauvoo. Bennett was not only a physician, but also a veteran of the U.S. Army and quartermaster general of Illinois. Smith immediately seized upon the potential political influence that Bennett might bring to the new city and personally baptized him into the faith. Bennett proved a capable leader and soon won the trust of the prophet.[34]

At the time of their meeting, Smith was drafting the Nauvoo City Charter, a document giving unprecedented power and autonomy to the city. The charter made Nauvoo a virtual city-state under the firm control of the Mormon prophet. This political arrangement would ensure a degree of autonomy and security for the Mormons that they were unable to attain in their former homes. No longer would local or state officials interfere with Mormon plans. To demonstrate his political influence, Bennett personally presented the document to state lawmakers. The Illinois legislature, in an attempt to cater to the growing Mormon population, gave Bennett all that he requested without a single dissenting vote.[35]

The Nauvoo City Charter also allowed Smith the power to protect his most controversial doctrine: polygamy. As early as 1835, Smith began the practice of plural marriage.[36] Realizing that polygamy would undoubtedly increase the persecution heaped upon the church, Smith kept the practice a secret from outsiders as well as from the main body of the church for several years. Rumors eventually spread throughout both Mormon and Gentile communities in the state. In Nauvoo it was rumored that Bennett not only embraced the Mormon practice of polygamy but had several unmarried mistresses as well.[37] In the sometimes confusing moral standards of Nauvoo, a plural marriage performed under the authority of the prophet was considered a most honorable thing, while a man taking an additional wife without the consent of the church was deemed adulterous.[38] For the time being Smith chose to ignore the evidence of Bennett's philandering. He was basking in his greatest victory and had further need of Bennett's military and political skills.

Smith proved himself a mediocre military leader while in Missouri and Ohio. Nonetheless he realized that an army would be essential to defending the newly awarded freedoms granted in the Nauvoo City Charter. Boatloads of new converts, coming up the Mississippi River, arrived at a rate that must have pleased the prophet. Five thousand immigrants came from Great Britain alone between 1840 and 1845.[39] These predominantly working-class people brought with them many skills necessary for the building up of the Kingdom of God in Nauvoo. They also brought the manpower for a sizeable army. Smith lacked the knowledge and experience to muster an army of such numbers from his increasingly diverse followers.

Smith again turned to Bennett for help. Bennett's experience in both the U.S. Army and the Illinois state militia proved vital to the organization of the city's military force. The Nauvoo City Charter gave Smith the power to raise a volunteer army, which he named the Nauvoo Legion.[40] To secure his place at the head of this army, Smith petitioned the governor of Illinois and received the rank of lieutenant general. Using the most liberal interpretations of the charter, Smith and Bennett began conscripting the men of Nauvoo. The ranks swelled, and soon the Nauvoo Legion was the largest army in Illinois. In 1844 there were more than five thousand adult members of the legion with at least five hundred youths in regimented auxiliaries. Smith at last had a formidable army to defend his work.[41]

"Lieutenant-General" Joseph Smith Reviewing the Nauvoo Legion.
Courtesy The Church of Jesus Christ of Latter-day Saints

The legion frequently drilled and paraded throughout the city and surrounding areas. The Mormon army impressed many people in Illinois, and several non-Mormons in neighboring towns even opted to drill with the Nauvoo Legion rather than join their own local militia groups. This defection caused friction with the leaders of other towns in Hancock County.[42]

This conflict only marked the latest problem to emerge from the region. Nauvoo was now rivaling Chicago in size.[43] While Smith stopped short of overtly dictating the Mormon vote, members of the church tended to vote as a block. The older non-Mormon communities of Warsaw and Carthage began feeling their own political power and influence waning in Hancock County and in Springfield. Social differences between the Mormons and their neighbors raised problems in Illinois just as they had in New York, Ohio, and Missouri. In spite of official denials from the church leadership, continued rumors of the Mormon practice of polygamy were spreading around the state. To make matters worse, Smith and Bennett clashed openly in the new city.

Many Mormons in Nauvoo had been suspicious of Bennett from the beginning. Smith ignored the rumors until one day, when the legion was enacting a mock battle, Bennett reportedly tried to murder him in the resulting melee. Faced with this and other charges related to adultery, Bennett eventually fled Nauvoo. In the communities already angered by the rise of Mormon power, Bennett discovered a new set of allies. The "anti-Mormons," as they were called, quickly supported Bennett's cause. He began work on a damaging, highly exaggerated, and deceptive series of letters about Nauvoo called "The History of the Saints; or, An Exposé of Joe Smith and Mormonism." Newspapers across the country published the sensational letters. In them Bennett claimed that he had joined the Mormon hierarchy in order to expose their systematic murder and prostitution. His lurid and fantastical accounts eventually made most eastern newspapers discount his work. The damage in Illinois, however, was irreversible.[44]

Bennett saw to it that the Mormons would soon be subject to all the same charges and actions that they had suffered in New York, Ohio, and Missouri. The Illinois Democratic Party was so embarrassed by its association with the Mormons that the leaders quickly named Thomas Ford, a man devoid of sympathies for the religion, as a gubernatorial candidate.[45] This left Smith alienated from state politics once again. To make matters worse, the Bennett articles inspired a new wave of Mormon hatred in Missouri. Politicians began to call for the extradition of Smith back to their state. When an unknown assailant tried to murder Governor Boggs of Missouri, the wounded governor accused Smith of sponsoring the attack.[46] The prophet surrounded himself with bodyguards and often went into hiding. His days in Illinois were numbered. He needed a new home and a fresh start for his people, but where?

By 1844 both Sam Houston and Joseph Smith knew that they needed to make major changes for the survival of their respective peoples. Houston placed his hopes in annexation by the United States. Barring that possibility, he knew that he desperately needed help in the physical defense of his nation. Smith, on the other hand, needed somewhere to settle where he could govern his people free from outside interference. As news from Texas began filtering up the Mississippi River to Nauvoo, Smith began looking into options for autonomy involving the Texas Republic.

CHAPTER 3

Mormon Interest in the Texas Republic, 1842–44

Eighteen forty-four was a pivotal year for the Mormons in Nauvoo. Their well-being was threatened in ways reminiscent of their persecution in Missouri. Residents of surrounding towns were calling for the forced expulsion of the Mormons from the state.[1] After they had struggled for five years to build a great city in the swamps of the Mississippi River, mob rule once again threatened the Mormon Saints.

Smith was not one to sit back and watch lawless mobs destroy his life's masterwork. He quickly came up with several plans for the protection of his religion, his people, and his way of life. Three of Smith's most ambitious plans directly involved the Texas Republic. These plans were, first, to run for president of the United States on a platform of Texas annexation; second, to raise an army to patrol the Texas and Oregon frontiers; and, third, to move the main body of the church from Illinois to the Texas-Mexico border and establish an independent nation.[2]

There are several reasons why Smith might look to Texas for a solution to his problems. The first reason, as mentioned earlier, deals with the unique opportunities available in the Republic at that time. Second, Texas would obviously provide a familiar Euro-American culture, yet be free of the laws of the United States that had worked to the detriment of the church. Third, the Mormons seemed to have a general interest in what was happening in the Texas Republic. Finally, Texas had religious significance for Mormons because of its archaeology, anthropology, and proximity to Native American and Mexican populations. The latter two reasons warrant further analysis to help explain Smith's desire to become involved in Texas affairs.

During the 1840s the people of Nauvoo were well aware of situations in the Texas Republic. Smith had sent a church elder to Texas as early as 1843.[3] In addition, both the Mormons' secular and religious newspapers carried articles describing many aspects of the young republic. The sheer number of articles in their small newspapers shows that there was a great interest in what was going on in Texas. This might be explained as reflecting a general interest in Texas throughout the United States at this time. It is significant to note, however, that the Oregon Territory emerged as a popular topic in the news of the time, yet Texas articles outnumbered Oregon articles in Nauvoo newspapers. Perhaps there was something in the perceived character of Texas and Texans that made the Mormons interested in the Republic. After all, Mormons, like the Texans, considered themselves an independent and singular people.

The first secular newspaper of Nauvoo, the *Wasp*, which ran from April, 1842, to April, 1843, put out fifty-one issues. It was a small, four-page newspaper made up mostly of articles from more-sophisticated eastern newspapers. During its one-year run it printed at least eighteen articles devoted to happenings in Texas, an average of more than one article every three weeks. A sampling of articles from the *Wasp* shows the impressions the Mormons of Nauvoo would have received in the two years prior to the Mormon negotiations with Texas.

In the spring of 1842 the *Wasp* ran two articles quoting Houston's appeals for peace, as well as threats of war against Mexico. Houston said,

> You threaten to conquer Texas—we will war with Mexico. Your pretensions with ours you have refered [*sic*] to the social world and to the God of battles—we refer our cause to the same tribunals. The issue involves the fate of nations—destiny must determine—its course is only known to the tribunals of heaven . . . Our incentives will not be a love of conquest—it will be to disarm tyranny of its power.[4]

The words of Houston, drawing upon the same religious imagery at times used by Smith, would have touched the hearts of the Mormons, who also saw themselves unjustly threatened on all sides.[5]

During that summer of 1842 the Mormons in Nauvoo read how Antonio López de Santa Anna forced loans from the Catholic church to fund his war with Texas.[6] These actions would not endear General Santa

Anna to a religion that had suffered a two-million-dollar loss of property at the hands of the bigoted leaders of Missouri. Mormons also read how the Texas Congress had declared war on Mexico only to have Houston veto the action.[7] This action no doubt impressed the Mormons, who practiced a high level of military vigilance while preferring time and again to maintain peace.

In the spring of 1843, the *Nauvoo Neighbor* replaced the *Wasp* as Nauvoo's secular newspaper. Interest in Texas continued to grow, as is reflected in this newspaper's content. In its first fifteen months of circulation, the *Nauvoo Neighbor* ran at least thirty-six Texas-related articles at an average of an article every two weeks. Texas articles published in the *Nauvoo Neighbor* during 1843 and 1844 were diverse, varying from annexation issues, to troubles with Mexico, to an editorial on the Bowie knife.[8]

Given the theocratic nature of Nauvoo, one might initially suspect that Smith may have manipulated the city's newspapers to forward his agenda.[9] Therefore the increase of Texas articles might be seen as an attempt to garner interest in his Texas plans. A closer look at chronology, however, reveals just the opposite. Smith's Texas plans seem to have been affected by the articles he himself was reading from Nauvoo newspapers or directly from Texas and eastern newspapers that came up the Mississippi River. So rather than his influencing the news, it seems that the newspapers were actually influencing Smith in his plans.[10]

Of Smith's three plans involving the Texas Republic, the most ambitious was to run for president of the United States. This endeavor would have ensured fair treatment of the Mormons in Nauvoo and elsewhere in the United States. Smith had learned in his years of leadership how to manipulate the political system to his advantage. He was a master at playing the Whigs and Democrats against each other for the short-term benefit of the Saints.[11] Perhaps he could manipulate this system at the federal level. Smith's only chance of winning the election was to split the Electoral College three ways and hope for a presidential appointment from the House of Representatives.[12] Smith clearly believed this was a possibility. In a campaign speech delivered on March 7, 1844, he said, "When I look into the Eastern papers and see how popular I am, I am afraid I shall be President."[13]

Smith organized his missionary force not only to make converts, but also to educate Americans on the issues he represented.[14] One of his biggest issues was the annexation of Texas. During that same March 7, 1844, campaign speech, Smith defined his views. He first made it clear that he was for the annexation of the Texas Republic to the United States. An abolitionist, Smith proposed, "As soon as Texas was annexed, I would liberate the slaves in two or three States, indemnifying their owners, and send the negroes to Texas, and from Texas to Mexico, where all colors are alike."[15] This view was not his original thinking; rather he was echoing the views of leading abolitionists of his time.[16]

Smith then warned against the dangers of allowing Great Britain a foothold in Texas: "The first thing they would do, if they got possession, would be to set the negroes and the Indians to fight, and they would use us up. . . . It will be more honorable for us to receive Texas and set the negroes free, and use the negroes and the Indians against our foes."[17] This idea of raising an army in the frontier would again become an issue in a later plan involving the Texas Republic.

Smith concluded his campaign speech with a prophetic warning:

> Don't let Texas go, lest our mothers and daughters of the land should laugh us in the teeth; and if these things are not so, God never spoke by any prophet since the world began. How much better is it for the nation to bear a little expense than to have the Indians and British upon us and destroy us all. We should grasp all the territory we can . . . And if it was not sufficient, I would call upon Canada, and annex it.[18]

As mentioned earlier in the speech, Smith introduced the idea of an army of Native Americans and freed African American slaves to protect the frontier against British encroachment in the West. This idea led to his second plan involving Texas: a volunteer army to police the frontier between Texas and Oregon. Two weeks after the annexation speech, an article in the March 20, 1844, issue of the *Nauvoo Neighbor* mentioned the difficulties of travel in New Mexico because of hostile tribes of Native Americans. The territory seemed to be promising for Americans only if settlers could travel unmolested through it. Significantly, on the day following this issue of the newspaper, Smith records that he called a meeting with his council for "discussing the privilege of raising troops to protect the making of settlements in the uncivilized portions of our continent."[19] It seems that Smith caught the vision of manifest destiny and saw his possible role in it.

During the next few days the plan evolved and then solidified in Smith's mind. On March 26 he approved a memorial to Congress that read in part,

> Whereas, many of the citizens of these United States have migrated, and are migrating to Texas, Oregon, and other lands contiguous to this nation; and whereas, Texas has declared herself free and independent, without the necessary power to protect her rights and liberties . . . Be it ordained by the Senate and House of Representatives of the United States of America, in Congress assembled, that Joseph Smith, of the city of Nauvoo, in the State of Illinois, is hereby authorized and empowered to raise a company of one hundred thousand armed volunteers, in the United States and Territories.[20]

That weekend he signed the memorial and sent it to Washington, D.C., with his ambassador to the United States, Orson Hyde.[21]

Smith's third, and most radical, plan also dealt with the Texas Republic. Unlike his other two schemes, this plan was kept in strictest secrecy among the top leadership of the church and was to be enacted only if Smith's presidential campaign failed. Smith proposed the relocation of the church to the Texas Republic in order to organize an autonomous government run by the Mormons themselves. Considering the recent emergence of nations during this time, especially the attempt at the Republic of the Rio Grande in 1840, it seemed that anything was possible in the Texas-Mexico borderlands.

Spiritually speaking, a homeland on the Texas-Mexico border would also be important to the Latter-day Saints. To comprehend the full implications of Smith's Texas plan, one must first understand the Mormon concept of race. According to the Book of Mormon, indigenous Americans were "Lamanites," the descendants of the biblical tribe of Joseph and heirs to the blessings of Israel.[22] The book is filled with promises and warnings given by Native American prophets to their modern-day posterity. Typical in the Book of Mormon is this scripture, claimed by Smith to be written by an ancient American prophet named Alma: "For there are many promises which is [sic] extended to the Lamanites: for it is because of the traditions of their fathers that causeth them to remain in their state of ignorance; therefore the Lord will be merciful to them. . . . For behold, the promises of the Lord are extended to the Lamanites."[23] In addition Smith maintained that he had received additional revelations regarding the current state of Native Americans. The following prophecy, given in 1831, represents one of the dozens of revelations Smith made: "Before the great day of the Lord shall come . . . the Lamanites shall blossom as the rose."[24]

As mentioned earlier, Smith took it upon himself to spread his gospel to the Native American people around him. As a result the Mormons typically had better relationships with indigenous Americans than did others of European stock.[25] While this attitude may have helped Mormons in dealing with Native Americans, it only served to increase suspicion toward the Mormons by their Euro-American neighbors.

Mormons of that time claimed that the contemporary Mexican was in fact a Lamanite.[26] Therefore Mormons viewed Mexicans with a degree of respect and fraternity uncommon for Euro-Americans of that time. During the early 1840s it should be noted that actual contact between Mormons and Mexicans would have been scarce, and thus Mormons would have drawn their conclusions about Mexicans through folklore and accounts in the press. The *Wasp*, the *Nauvoo Neighbor*, and the Mormon religious newspaper the *Times and Seasons* all ran articles about Mexico and Mexicans outside the Texas context. These articles varied from discussions on antiquities to travelogues. There was nothing particularly bigoted or critical in these articles. Negative writings about Mexicans tended to be in reprints from articles originating in Texas.[27]

Another issue in early Mormon and Mexican relations was the almost exclusive practice of Roman Catholicism among the Mexican people. Most Mormons had converted from Protestant denominations in the eastern United States and northwestern Europe. Since the founding of the religion, most persecution leveled at the church came from Protestants. Alienated from their Protestant roots, Mormons would not necessarily have felt the animosity toward Roman Catholicism that many Protestants did.

Theological teachings of the time also instructed Mormons that the line of authority claimed by the Roman Catholic church was indeed correct. Smith taught, however, that the excesses and abuses of the early popes had negated the true authority of God in the religion. He also taught that Protestants were even further from the true authority of God since they had broken away from the Roman Catholics.[28] When Smith drafted legislation granting religious freedom to all of Nauvoo's inhabitants, the Catholics were significantly mentioned first on the list.[29]

During the 1840s Mormons were apparently not as influenced by the racial and religious prejudices common among other Euro-Americans at the time.[30] This attitude varied at times as the Mormons eventually moved into the Great Basin of Northern Mexico under the leadership of Brigham Young. By and large, though, Mormons maintained positive relations with Mexico even after moving into the Southwest. By the late nineteenth century, Mexican president Porfirio Díaz went so far as to allow several settlements of Mormons to be established in the Mexican states of Sonora and Chihuahua. The Díaz government even turned a blind eye to the illicit Mormon practice of polygamy.[31]

Also telling of Mormon attitudes toward Mexicans was the Mormon response to the U.S.–Mexican War. In 1846 a battalion of five hundred soldiers was conscripted from Mormon refugees headed to Mexican territory surrounding the Great Salt Lake. Before the battalion left for the war, Young commanded the Mormon soldiers:

> Hold sacred the property of the people, never taking anything that does not belong to you only in case of starvation; though you may be traveling in an enemy's country, do not disturb fruit orchards or chicken coops or beehives, do not take anything but what you pay for—although it is customary for soldiers to plunder their enemies in time of war, it is wrong—always spare life when possible.[32]

Since the Mormons clearly had sympathies for the Mexicans in 1846, while technically at war with them, it is likely that these feelings were also common just two years earlier.

Smith's interest in moving to Texas was part of a greater plan that also included the possibility of moving to Oregon or Upper California. He may have first considered the move to Texas in February, 1844. At this time he organized an expedition to search the disputed Oregon Territory and Mexican lands in Upper California for potential places of settlement.

Smith was not yet ready to abandon his work in Nauvoo, but he was looking for safer places where he could send converts. On February 20, 1844, he commissioned a group of Mormon explorers to search Oregon and Upper California for appropriate places "where we can build a city in a day, and have a government of our own, get up into the mountains, where the devil cannot dig us out, and live in a healthful climate, where we can live as old as we have a mind to."[33]

Optimistic news from Texas buoyed the Mormons' spirit. The *Nauvoo Neighbor* printed articles about how the Republic was beginning to thrive agriculturally, with "every kind of produce cheap and abundant."[34] According to a reprint of an article in the *Texas Telegraph*, recently discovered Native American ruins were clearly the "castles or temples" of earlier inhabitants of the land. The accompanying Mormon editorial claimed this to be evidence of the validity of the Book of Mormon.[35] Smith must have been thrilled to find what he considered proof of his work so close to home.[36]

And in a more practical vein Smith would have been intrigued by the *Nauvoo Neighbor*'s first reports of Texas colonies established with the cooperation of the Republic. On February 7, 1844, the newspaper ran a front-page article compiled from two Texas newspapers reporting on favorable conditions to be found in Texas.[37] Commerce was flourishing and immigrants were thriving. It also included the story of unnamed German colonists who came destitute to the Republic but who were now prospering in Austin and on the Colorado River:[38]

> Most of them brought nothing to the country with them, but their families; all their means being exhausted by their arrival. But they still retained a fund which nothing, save disease and bodily infirmity could render unavailable—their industry, skill and energy—their moral feelings, habits and common sense—all the funds necessary to acquire everything in Texas.[39]

The Mormons viewed themselves as having these same characteristics. Could they not also thrive in the young republic? So perhaps it is significant that two weeks after this article was printed Smith organized the exploring party that was to travel to Oregon and Upper California via the Texas Republic.

Nauvoo Temple, Nauvoo, Illinois (daguerrotype) © by Intellectual
Reserve, Inc. *Courtesy of Family and Church History Department,
The Church of Jesus Christ of Latter-day Saints.*

On February 15, 1844, one of Smith's senior apostles, Lyman Wight,
wrote a letter from Wisconsin, where he was milling lumber for constructing the Mormons' most sacred building—the Nauvoo Temple.[40]
He was having trouble purchasing lumber from the local Menominee
tribe of Native Americans because of an uncooperative federal agent.
Members of the tribe had suggested that the Mormons help them move

to Texas where they would be free of federal control. This caused Wight to consider a similar plan for the Saints:

> A few of us here have arrived at this conclusion in our minds . . . that as the Gospel has not been fully opened in all the South and Southwestern States, as also Texas, Mexico, Brazil, &c., together with the West Indian Islands . . . also having an influence over the Indians, so as to induce them to sell their lands to the United States, and go to a climate southwest . . . we have in our minds to go to the table-lands of Texas, to a point we may find to be the most eligible, there locate, and let it be a place of gathering for all the South.[41]

Wight followed up that correspondence with a private letter addressed to Smith that same day:

> The committee is well informed of the Cherokee and Choctaw nations that live between the state of Arkansas and the Colorado river of the Texans, owning large plantations and thousands of slaves, and they are also very desirous to have an interview with the Elders of this Church, upon the principles of the Book of Mormon.[42]

Wight reasoned that the prophet, devoted to proselytizing the Native Americans, would view this as a choice opportunity. In addition he pointed out that Texas could be a gathering place for the thousands of slave-holding southern converts that he expected would join the church.[43]

According to Smith's journal, he received the letters on March 10, 1844.[44] Intrigued by Wight's suggestion, he decided to convene a council to discuss the Texas proposal. This would be the first meeting of a highly secretive group called "The Kingdom of God and His Laws with the keys and powers thereof and judgement in the hands of his servants."[45] This rather drawn-out name was commonly shortened to the Council of Fifty since it consisted of fifty men. Regarding the Council of Fifty's plans for Texas, Smith's journal reads:

> Letter was read from Wight and others Dated Feb 15 1844 to B Young, W Richards, &c. About removing to the table lands of Saxet [Texas] &c. &c. . . . Joseph asked, can this council keep what I say, not make it

public, all held up their hands. . . . Send 25 men by the yrenip [pinery] through to Antas Fee [Santa Fe] &c., and if Notsuoh [Houston] will embrace the gospel . . . can amend that constitution and make it the voice of Jehovah and shame the US.[46]

Following the reverse code of Smith's scribe, the meaning of these notes is quickly deciphered. The Mormon hierarchy planned to dispatch a party from Wight's pinery to meet with Houston, teach him the Mormon gospel, and discuss the possibility of purchasing land to settle a group of the Saints.

The details of this meeting were left intentionally vague. The Council of Fifty remains to this day somewhat of a mystery to Mormon scholars and western historians.[47] All official minutes kept by this group, except for one meeting in 1880, either were burned or are kept locked in a vault in Salt Lake City.[48]

What is known about the Council of Fifty is that their meetings were part of a plan to establish a political "Kingdom of God" in the United States. Smith ordained himself "king" of the Kingdom of God and expected to serve in that role until the second coming of Jesus Christ. From the Mormon perspective the Kingdom of God was the temporal government that the Mormons established to rule over themselves and eventually, in their view, the world.[49] Although built upon the teachings and principles of the religion, the Council of Fifty was not exclusively Mormon. At the time of its organization three members of the council were not Latter-day Saints, although they were obviously sympathetic to the Mormon cause.[50]

Exploring the possibility of establishing the Kingdom of God in Texas was the first order of business of the Council of Fifty. Although the official records of this initial meeting are unavailable, one key player in the council later wrote detailed memoirs of the activities of the group. His name was George Miller. Miller wrote that the primary goal of the church was to get Smith elected as president of the United States. If that failed, the Council of Fifty

. . . would then send a minister to the then Republic of Texas to make a treaty with the Cabinet of Texas for all that country north of a west line from the falls of the Colorado River to the Nueces; thence down the same to the Gulf of Mexico, and along the same to Rio Grande, and up the same to the United States territory, and get them to acknowledge us as a nation; and on the part of the Church we would help them defend themselves against Mexico, standing as a go-between the belligerent powers. . . . Lucien Woodworth was chosen minister to Texas, and I was to return to the pineries to bring down Wight.[51]

While the Mormon ambassador, Woodworth, prepared to leave for Texas, Nauvoo received a number of conflicting reports about the state of affairs in the Republic. An overly optimistic article reprinted from the *Houston Telegraph* claimed that annexation to the United States was a foregone conclusion. The Texan author wrote, "Ere another harvest is gathered in Texas, the broad banner of Washington may be unfurled in glory on our western border, and the burnished arms of American troops will be reflected from the sparkling waters of the Nueces. Westward! The star of empire takes its way!"[52] It is not known the impact this news had on the Mormon plans for negotiations with the Texas Republic. While this would have supported Smith's presidential agenda, it would also have prevented plans for establishing an independent nation in the Texas frontier. Smith could perhaps attempt negotiations with the federal government, but his earlier experiences in Washington, D.C., left him with a cynical view of that option.[53]

Although the annexation of Texas may have seemed certain to the *Houston Telegraph*, events in the East were bringing the negotiations to a halt. On February 28, U.S. Secretary of State Abel Upshur was killed in an artillery explosion aboard the USS *Princeton*.[54] Secretary Upshur had favored annexation, and this upheaval in the government stalled the process for several more months. The Council of Fifty saw this as a divine act. Brigham Young exclaimed, "The Lord is cutting off the bitterest branches. Look at the explosion of the big gun on board the Princeton war-steamer at Washington. God will deliver his faithful Saints."[55]

In further support of the Texas Kingdom of God, another newspaper from Texas reached Smith; it claimed that the annexation report from the prior edition of the *Houston Telegraph* was a hoax. With hopes lifted, the Mormon ambassador, Woodworth, left Nauvoo for Austin on March 14, 1844.[56] A few days later, the front page of the *Nauvoo Neighbor* declared to the people of Nauvoo that the annexation article was a fraud. The article

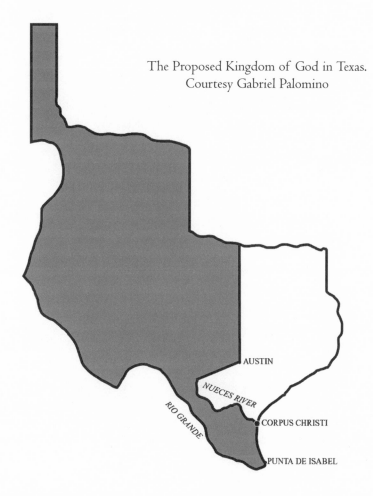

The Proposed Kingdom of God in Texas.
Courtesy Gabriel Palomino

AUSTIN

NUECES RIVER

RIO GRANDE

CORPUS CHRISTI

PUNTA DE ISABEL

stated that many Texans were not ready to give up their autonomy until they tried further negotiations with Mexico for peace. In addition Mexicans in Santa Fe were reported to be joining the Texans.[57] With characteristic optimism the Council of Fifty must have believed that the powers of heaven were conspiring to their support.

During this time Orson Hyde, the Mormon ambassador to the United States, continued to promote Smith's presidential run and his volunteer army of the West. Communication remained slow on the frontier, and Smith pressed on with what little information he could glean from letters from his ambassadors and newspapers coming up the Mississippi River.

While his own newspaper praised his views on annexation, Smith read an article that made him think positively about the prospects of a Texas Kingdom of God. On April 10, 1844, the *Nauvoo Neighbor* reprinted a letter written by former president Andrew Jackson:

> Remember, also, that if annexed to the United States, our western boundary would be the Rio Grande, which is of itself a fortification on account of its extensive, barren and uninhabitable plains. With such a barrier on our west we are invincible. The whole European world could not in combination against us, make an impression upon our Union.
>
> From the Rio Grande, over land, a large army could not march, or be supplied, unless from the Gulf by water, which by vigilance, could always be intercepted; and to march an army near the gulf they could be harassed by militia, and detained till an organized force could be raised to meet them.

If by some chance Ambassador Woodworth gained success in his negotiations with Sam Houston, the Rio Grande would become the southern and western boundary of the Mormon Kingdom of God. The five-thousand-strong Nauvoo Legion could defend these lands adequately against a larger force. Besides, was not the Mormon capital of Nauvoo a river city built from the swamps and wastelands of the Mississippi River? The Rio Grande promised to be a familiar environment for the kingdom-building Mormons.

While Ambassador Woodworth met with Houston, Texas annexation dominated the news in Nauvoo. Four stories on Texas annexation appeared in the *Nauvoo Neighbor* on April 10. By comparison, the Semi-Annual Conference of the Church, a very significant ecclesiastical event, received only one paragraph of coverage. In that same newspaper came news that the hated Missourians were relocating in large numbers to the Pacific Coast. It would be difficult for the Latter-day Saints to make a fresh start with their old enemies as neighbors. This news made Texas an even more desirable and likely location for the new home of the church.

Allowing for travel time, Smith must have known that Woodworth was in Texas by early April. It was a tense and exciting time in Nauvoo. The hope of an independent state where the Saints could create their own society and government was tempered by the fears and threats of mobs and militia. Although Smith still considered other options for his church, it seemed that a Texas Kingdom of God continued to be a strong possibility. All would depend on Woodworth's negotiations with Houston. In Nauvoo, Smith and the Council of Fifty waited anxiously for news from Texas.

CHAPTER 4

The Texas~Mormon Negotiations of 1844

No historian has yet uncovered any Texas documents at all or any primary documents in general related to Lucien Woodworth's stay in Austin. Obviously the negotiations were handled in strictest secrecy. Had Antonio López de Santa Anna known what the Mormons were proposing, he might have sent troops across the Rio Bravo to stop any further occupation of the land. One can only guess Houston's reaction to meeting an emissary from one of the United States' most maligned religions who was offering to purchase three-fourths of the Republic. It would have served Houston well not to let other Texans know he was entertaining such a guest. These were desperate times in Texas, and Houston was not above secret negotiations.[1]

The exact timing for the Mormon proposal was perhaps a little awkward. During the second week of April, a Texas delegation proposed to sign a preliminary treaty of annexation with the United States.[2] Although the treaty negotiations gave some glimmer of hope for annexation, they did little to guarantee the survival of the Republic if the U.S. Congress persisted in rejecting it. Houston feared that this constant vacillation would weaken Texas in dealing with England, France, and Mexico.[3] On April 14, Houston wrote his secretary of state, Anson Jones, "If annexation is not effected at the present session of Congress ... call upon the English and French ministers and ascertain the prospect of all those Governments giving us a guarantee against further molestation from Mexico and an indefinite truce. We cannot be trifled within the present crisis of our affairs."[4] Texas, it seemed, was willing to deal with whoever could help in her present crisis.

The specifics of the meetings between Woodworth and Houston remain unknown. Fortunately George Miller witnessed Woodworth's report to the Council of Fifty following his return home on May 2, 1844, and recorded what transpired in his memoirs:[5] "The council convened to hear his report. It was altogether as we could wish it. On the part of the church there was [sic] commissioners appointed to meet the Texas Congress, to sanction or ratify the said treaty, partly entered into by our minister and the Texas Cabinet."[6]

Without revealing the exact details of the agreement, Miller made it clear that Houston and Woodworth reached a preliminary understanding about the purchase of certain Texas lands. But what territory did the Mormons expect to get from Texas? As previously mentioned, the territory the Mormons initially asked for amounted to approximately three-quarters of the Republic. Granted that this territory was at that time among the least valuable lands in Texas, still it seems highly unlikely that Houston would have consented to making that large a concession. In light of Texas historical documents it was clearly not a possibility. As early as May 6, 1844, Houston began drawing up plans for a greater Texas which would stretch to the Pacific Ocean.[7] The Mormons' plan for the Kingdom of God in the western and northern reaches of the Republic would interfere with Houston's vision.

Obviously Houston would have rejected Woodworth's initial offer to buy the greater part of the Republic. Still the Texas president must have entertained the idea of using the Nauvoo Legion to defend his weak southern border at no expense to his government. It seems likely that Houston then made a counteroffer. While existing documents do not definitively say which lands they discussed, clues exist as to what settlements were agreed upon. Key to this is an entry in the *Journal History of the Church of Jesus Christ of Latter-day Saints* dated April 2, 1847. The entry reads, "Bishop George Miller gave his views about the Church removing to Texas, to the country lying between the Nueces and Rio Grande rivers."[8]

A letter that George Miller wrote to Brigham Young a month earlier also supports this contention. He discussed settling "on the Camanshee [Comanche] lands on the eastern side of the Cordilleras Mountains [Southern Rockies] so far south that we could grow cotton and even sugarcane . . . we could get sea-coast on the Gulph [sic] of Mexico, where we could land emigrants from the States of England, France, Germany, Norway, etc. in our own ports."[9]

These descriptions, although given some time after the negotiations, clearly show that the land Houston considered selling to the Mormons consisted of the disputed Nueces strip between Texas and Mexico. This land had given Houston the most trouble because it was sparsely populated by Texans and thus hard to defend. By allowing the Mormons to establish their Kingdom of God in this region, he would lose territory but in turn create a buffer nation between Texas and Mexico. The southern, isolated location of the Nueces Strip would also not interfere with his establishment of a greater Texas. This mirrored the same logic that prompted Texans to support the establishment of the Republic of the Rio Grande and the potential settlement of French colonists on some of the same lands just a few years earlier.

The ports on the Gulf of Mexico mentioned during the negotiations most likely were the frontier outposts of Corpus Christi on the Nueces River, El Fronton de Santa Isabel near the Rio Grande, and La Isla Brazos de Santiago on the southern end of the Laguna Madre.[10] Houston apparently conducted some skillful boosterism since these so-called ports remained little more than primitive settlements in 1844. Woodworth was either oblivious of this fact or not intimidated by the austere conditions of frontier Texas.

Woodworth accepted Houston's counteroffer. It is easy to understand why Houston agreed to deal with the Mormons: as long as he could put a large, friendly population between himself and Mexico, the Republic could thrive. In order for Santa Anna to send an invading force from Matamoros or Laredo or any of his favorite crossing points in southern Texas, he would now have to contend with five thousand soldiers from the Nauvoo Legion. The stability the legion could provide the Republic was well worth giving up lands that Texas controlled only on paper. In addition this increased security on the southern border would give Houston leverage and allow him more time to negotiate favorable annexation terms with the United States.

George Miller's account then named the three commissioners chosen to lead the final negotiations with the Texas Congress. The appointed commissioners mentioned in the record were Woodworth, George Miller, and Almon Babbitt.[11] The lack of documentation in Texas archives makes

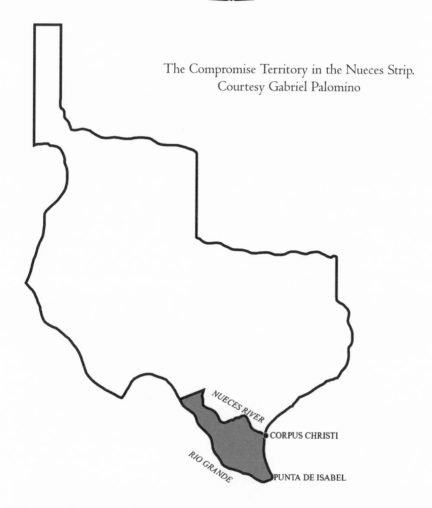

The Compromise Territory in the Nueces Strip.
Courtesy Gabriel Palomino

it unlikely that the Texas Congress had any idea that they would be meeting with representatives of the Church of Jesus Christ of Latter-day
Saints. This fact alone makes it clear that Houston considered the sale of
the Nueces Strip to the Mormons a contingency plan, in the event his
negotiations with the United States the following week went awry.
Should no help be forthcoming from the United States, he could then
sell the Nueces Strip to the Mormons, who would stabilize the region
with their population base and army.

Houston did not stand alone in dealing in duplicitous politics.
Although proceeding with the Texas negotiations in earnest, Smith also
used Texas as a contingency plan. After all, he persisted in his plan of

running for president of the United States, while at the same time exploring possibilities of relocating to Oregon or California. Smith had great respect for the U.S. Constitution and was at heart a patriot.[12] Just as he believed that modern Christianity had fallen away from the pure teachings of Christ, he felt that the United States had deviated from the original spirit of the Constitution.[13] This is why he could run for the office of president of the United States while privately preparing to leave the country. If he could not affect change in the United States through the political system, he "could but fall back on Texas, and be a kingdom notwithstanding."[14] Obviously, as with Houston, this treaty was not his first choice.

Assuming that the negotiations proved successful, Smith ordered George Miller and Lyman Wight to prepare to settle the new Mormon territory. Wight, an early Mormon convert, initially proposed moving his Wisconsin-based Black River Lumber Company to Texas because of problems with a federal Indian agent. He was a veteran of the War of 1812, a general in the Nauvoo Legion, and fiercely loyal to Smith. In 1838 he had surrendered himself with Smith to the Missouri state militia and had been ordered shot alongside his leader. When militia officers offered Wight freedom in exchange for testimony against the Mormon prophet, he replied bitterly, "Shoot and be damned!"[15] Clearly his deeds proved his unswerving loyalty to Smith. With a strong military background and skills in the milling of timber, he was an obvious choice for a Texas colonizer.

As alluded to in his letter to Smith, Wight and his lumber company were developing close ties with the local Menominee. Many members of the tribe expressed sympathy toward Wight and his company because of the persecution the Mormons had suffered at the hands of the white man.[16] They wept openly upon hearing about the persecution suffered by the Mormons in Ohio and Missouri and felt a kinship that only fellow victims could understand. The chiefs of the tribe even planned a council to discuss the mass conversion of the tribe to the Mormon faith.[17] Wight planned to remove his colony of approximately 150 Mormons from the mills near Indian Lands and resettle in Texas. Whether he intended to bring the Menominee tribe with him is unknown. It was certainly an option he considered.[18] Unlike in Ohio, Missouri, or Illinois, in this new land there would be no power to interfere with their fraternization with the Native Americans. Miller, in particular, had a strong sympathy for Native Americans and an equally strong hatred of the United States.[19]

If Smith did indeed win the presidential election, he would work for Texas annexation. That being the case, the Texas purchase might furnish another outpost for Mormon settlement. Wight's people could continue in their milling work in Texas and provide work and homes for the expected flow of Mormon European immigrants.[20] If Smith lost the election, the Mormons could begin relocating en masse to the Mormon lands between Mexico and the Texas Republic to establish their Kingdom of God.

Smith knew that if his Kingdom of God were to become a player on the world stage, he needed international support and recognition. This same reasoning is why Houston sought national recognition from the United States, England, and France. Smith duplicated Houston's strategy and named Mormon ambassadors to those three nations as well.[21] Since France and England had been quick to recognize Texas as an independent nation, it would follow that they might also be persuaded to offer support to the new Mormon nation.[22]

While no existing Mormon document mentions sending an ambassador to Mexico, a newspaper article of the time makes an interesting charge:

> An express has just arrived here from the city of Mexico, bringing the important intelligence that JOE SMITH, the celebrated Mormon Prophet, of the Latter-day Saints, has concluded a treaty with Santa Anna for the purchase of Texas; for which he agrees to assume ten millions of the Mexican debt to England, and has hypothecated the State of Illinois as collateral security for the faithful redemption of said debt. Commissioners have already been appointed to run the boundary line, &c. General Ampudia and Martin Perfecto de Cos are named on the part of Santa Anna, and PROPHET MILLER and tigertail on the part of JOE SMITH.[23]

The veracity of this article comes immediately into question. Besides there being no known Mormon document naming an ambassador to Mexico, there has been no discovery of Mexican documents supporting this claim. Such information may be part of the private Council of Fifty records, although it seems unlikely.

Still, the possibility that Smith sent an ambassador to Mexico cannot yet be ruled out. If the report is accurate, then it would seem that Smith could have been trying to play upon Santa Anna's fears of Texas to win Mexican support for his Mormon theocratic state. Mexicans were not the only ones crossing the border during this time. Texans also wreaked havoc south of the Rio Grande, including a raid on the Mexican town of Mier ten miles south of Roma, Texas.[24] A Mormon buffer state might prove equally advantageous to Santa Anna.

The other problem with the article is the fact that it had originated in Iowa. Just across the Mississippi River from Nauvoo, many Iowans shared the feelings of their anti-Mormon neighbors in Illinois. The Iowa Democratic Party, which operated the newspaper, openly expressed antagonism toward the Mormons at the time. Charges such as those made in this article may have been an attempt to generate additional fear and hatred toward the Mormons. Not only had the Mormons been accused of forming secret alliances with African slaves and Native Americans, now they were consorting with the Mexicans. The result of such charges could only further damage the Mormons' standing in the state.

The three Mormon commissioners assigned to meet with the Texas Congress did not immediately leave for the Republic after receiving their assignments. Many reasons may explain why this was the case. Although Mormon assets were great in Illinois, they were not yet liquid and could only be used as the basis for a line of credit. Matters in Nauvoo also continued to be very complex that spring. Smith evaded several attempts by Missouri bounty hunters and police to arrest and extradite him.[25] Perhaps most significant, Smith may have been stalling to allow his other plans to develop.

The key to discerning the fate of his plans lay in the letters received from his ambassador to the United States, Orson Hyde. In May the first in a series of letters written by Ambassador Hyde arrived from Washington, D.C., addressed to the prophet. Things did not seem promising in Congress. In the politically charged election climate, no one seemed willing to present Congress with the Mormon memorial requesting authorization to raise the army of one hundred thousand volunteers, and thus the petition never reached the floor of Congress.[26] Ironically Smith received his first non-Mormon volunteer for his nonexistent frontier army just two weeks later.[27] Still Smith must have known that without congressional allies, his frontier army was a lost cause.

News about a possible move to Texas or the Pacific was more encouraging. Hyde wrote, "If the Saints possess the kingdom I think they will have to take it; and the sooner it is done the more easily it is accomplished. Your superior wisdom must determine whether to go to Oregon, to Texas, or to remain within these United States."[28] He then wrote in another letter, dated the same day, that he had an extended conversation with Illinois senator Stephen A. Douglas. Douglas informed Hyde that "he would resign his seat in Congress if he could command the force that Mr. Smith could, and would be on the march to the country in a month."[29] He then provided a clandestine government map of Oregon to Hyde to give to Smith upon his return to Nauvoo.[30]

After four more days of dealing with the president and Congress, Ambassador Hyde wrote a letter that painted a bleaker picture of Smith's plans. Not only was Smith's proposal of a volunteer army dismissed by Congress, his bid for president was also "passed off with a smile."[31] Realistically his only chance at a presidential victory was to split the Electoral College three ways and hope for a favorable vote in the House of Representatives.[32] Clearly, without support in Congress this would not happen. This realization must have dampened Smith's spirits.

With the volunteer army no longer a possibility and hopes for a presidential victory slim, Hyde addressed the Oregon and Texas plans. In sharp contrast to his glowing accounts of Oregon just four days earlier, Hyde wrote, "Oregon is a good way off, and not very good country when you arrive there. I have read something of its history since I left, and have also conversed with gentlemen who have been there. The Tax upon women and children in removing there, would be very severe indeed."[33]

The other problem was the large number of Missourians immigrating to Oregon that spring. Cornelius Gilliam, a well-known Mormon hater from Missouri, was in fact organizing a party immigrating to Oregon that very month.[34]

Texas, on the other hand, seemed quite a different story. The stalemate over annexation provided the perfect opportunity to move forward with the final negotiations with Houston and, eventually, the Texas Congress. Ambassador Hyde wrote:

> . . . as Texas will not be admitted into our Union, how would it do for you to write President Houston and ask him what encouragement he

could give us if we would commence an immediate emigration there, and supply him with 1, 2, 3, 4, or 5 thousand soldiers to help fight the battle, and then if Mexico would not acknowledge the independence of Texas, but continue to harass her by small parties, make one tremendous rush upon Mexico and capture and subdue the whole country. This would secure Texas, Mexico, and California. If Mexico should acknowledge the independence of Texas without bloodshed. Then we should have a delightful soil and climate, and an opportunity of extending our settlement into California. . . . Texas would be a central point for emigration, for the coming in and going out of elders.[35]

Clearly Hyde felt that the time was right for an immediate migration to Texas. Not only would the Mormons occupy the Nueces Strip, they would put the entire strength of the Nauvoo Legion behind the defense of the border. In a move that ran contrary to the defensive nature of Smith's military strategies, Hyde went so far as to suggest an offensive war against Mexico. Still he held out for the possibility of peaceful coexistence of the Mormons along the Rio Grande. In addition to bringing economic prosperity to the Mormons, this also would open the door to their growing ambitions in Upper California.[36]

Hyde did not see all as perfect in Texas. He wisely pointed out the problems the Mormons would have in starting their own nation:

If we were to get Texas, or rather go there under the most favorable circumstances which we have any reason to hope for. There is an army to support, and also a navy. An executive and legislative government. Ministers and consuls to all nations. Would not this enormous weight of taxation keep out capitalist [sic] and sink the infant government?

He then subtly criticized the excess optimism of Smith and the Council of Fifty and called for a more realistic consideration of the Texas plan. He concluded, however, by avowing his loyalty and his acquiescence to their judgment on the issue.[37] Apparently Hyde's warnings had some impact on Smith as he contemplated his options in Texas.

Throughout the late spring of 1844, the *Nauvoo Neighbor* seemed to echo Smith's confusion about Texas and Oregon. One article stressed the hardship inherent in immigrating the long distance to Oregon.[38] While a move to Oregon remained a possibility, it seemed more remote with each passing month. Texas too remained a difficult issue. The *Nauvoo Neighbor* ran several articles about Texas in June, 1844, that dealt with the usual annexation problems, as well as providing more explanation of the complex relationship of Texas with Mexico, France, and England. The news offered no clear clues as to which path the Mormon leadership should follow.[39]

By June fate began forcing Smith's hand in his policy decisions. He had immediate problems to deal with at home that required action. Torn by external military threats and internal dissension, Nauvoo was a city on the brink of disaster. In the midst of this, Smith made some unexplained moves regarding Texas. On June 20, 1844, he began entertaining a Texas land speculator, a "southern gentleman" named Dr. Southwick who came from Louisiana.[40] Southwick, although an honored guest of the prophet, could not have picked a more complex time to come to Nauvoo. The only thing that is known specifically from existing documents is that Dr. Southwick came to sell a large tract of Texas land to the Mormons.[41] He got much more than he expected.

Dr. Southwick was not the only Texas land speculator trying to win the favor of the Mormons. On June 3, 1844, another speculator, John H. Walton, wrote Smith from Galveston.[42] In his letter he offered to sell a large tract of land in northern Texas between the Red and Trinity rivers.[43] It is not known how these men knew that Smith was in the market for Texas lands. The greater mystery is why Smith was interested in purchasing lands other than those offered by Houston. Why would Smith entertain offers from private speculators rather than from the Texas government? A logical answer is that Smith was looking at the more desirable northern lands for settlement. Since Houston apparently would not sell lands other than the Nueces Strip, Smith would have to make private purchases. Although they would not have their own nation, the Latter-day Saints could hope for a favorable position as citizens of the Republic.

Walton's letter perhaps answers that question. He makes some rather optimistic statements about Smith's potential within the Republic:

> I need not point out to a mind as ambitious and discerning as yours the advantages which would certainly result to you from settlement of

such a tract in this country. Should you remove here with all your adherents, you would at once acquire the controlling vote of Texas, and might yourself aspire to and obtain any office in the Republic.

With upward of fifteen thousand followers, Smith could command a certain influence in the Republic. Certainly he could dominate regional politics in areas where the Mormons purchased land.

Another answer might lie in the location of the potential purchase. The land bordered the Red River, which was the southern boundary of Indian Territory. This would put the Mormons near the Cherokee Nation. Just that spring Wight had written Smith about Cherokee interest in learning about Mormonism. The Cherokee were a wealthy people by frontier standards. Certainly Smith could see spiritual as well as economic advantages to a close association with that tribe.

Walton continued with an invitation for Smith to bring his army to help conquer and subjugate Mexico for the glory of the "Anglo Saxon" race and Texas. Though his army was substantial by frontier standards, Smith always preferred a defensive posture. As much as "General" Smith loved the pomp and grandeur of military life, he had little stomach for violence. The appeal for a war of conquest would not have affected Smith. He harbored no ill feeling toward Mexico, a nation of people whose physical and spiritual redemption was a keystone of his theology.

Perhaps most attractive to Smith would have been Walton's promise that

> In Texas you will find no dense population to contend with, no bigots to oppress, no overwhelming power to crush you in your infancy, but a new field open to the enterprising pioneer ... where every hand would be extended to you in friendship, and when you and your adherents in stead [sic] of forming a small third party in an inferior State, would at once assume and retain a commanding influence in a Republic doubtless richer in resources than any country in the world.

This was much more in keeping with Smith's agenda. Although he expected his theocracy to spread to the far reaches of the globe, his main goal remained to find a place where his people could practice their religion in peace. His lofty aspirations and ambitious plans all served the ultimate need to protect his people.

It is likely that Smith, at the very end, shied away from the responsibility of maintaining and defending such a large nation. Hyde's last letter warned about the unforeseen difficulties in managing an independent nation. Perhaps Hyde's warning made Smith see that his plans extended beyond his abilities. It did not take a prophet to foresee that ownership of the Nueces Strip was going to be contested by Mexico.[44] Perhaps after careful consideration of all issues involved, Smith had backed down from his grand scheme of nation building. Maybe he could satisfy himself with a portion of the Texas Republic where he and his people could be left alone.[45]

Smith's intentions that last week of June, 1844, whatever they may have been, were overshadowed by more tragic events. When he ordered the destruction of the *Nauvoo Expositor*, a dissident newspaper, he gave the state of Illinois the excuse it had needed to arrest him. Gov. Thomas Ford had a warrant issued against Smith for treason.[46] Armed mobs and an unruly militia massed outside Nauvoo, waiting for the final confrontation with the Mormon leader. The Texas land speculator, Dr. Southwick, managed as a non-Mormon to infiltrate the meetings of the mobsters. He returned to Nauvoo with news that the mobs intended to kill the prophet.[47] He had earlier reported that a group of men brought a cannon on his steamboat and unloaded it at Warsaw, Illinois.[48] Considering that Warsaw contained many anti-Mormons, the news was grim indeed.

Believing that his presence in Nauvoo further endangered the lives of its citizens, Smith crossed the Mississippi River, intending to flee to the West. Rather than placating the mobs, his absence only emboldened their threats against the city. When Smith received word that his flight from the city had made things worse, he decided to surrender to the governor of Illinois.[49] When he had faced a similar situation only five years earlier in Missouri, his surrender had led to a death sentence and the expulsion of his people from the state. As he returned back across the Mississippi River, he experienced premonitions of his own death and claimed, "I am going like a lamb to the slaughter; but I am calm as a summer's morning; I have a conscience void of offense towards God, and towards all men. I shall die innocent, and it shall yet be said of me—he was murdered in cold blood."[50]

Last Public Address of Lieut. General Joseph Smith.
Courtesy The Church of Jesus Christ of Latter-day Saints

One of his last acts before surrendering was to send a horse for Dr. Southwick. In the confusion a Nauvoo legionnaire commandeered the horse for another use and Southwick remained in Nauvoo.[51] What business Smith proposed to settle with the land speculator can only be guessed. Was he trying to find an escape to Texas? Was he attempting a last-minute deal to purchase Texas lands for resettling the residents of Nauvoo? These questions will probably never be answered because Smith, his brother Hyrum, and two apostles—John Taylor and Willard Richards—soon became prisoners of the governor of Illinois.

As part of the terms of his surrender, Smith ordered the Nauvoo Legion disarmed.[52] Without providing for adequate protection for Smith or the city of Nauvoo, the governor left the prophet in the custody of militia in the neighboring town of Carthage, Illinois. On the afternoon of June 27, 1844, a mixture of militia and armed mobsters stormed the small jail holding Smith and other Mormon leaders. The four Mormons inside defended themselves with two canes and two small pistols that they had managed to smuggle into their cell earlier in the day. After a brief struggle the mob of 250 men overcame the four poorly armed Mormons. When the smoke cleared, the thirty-eight-year-old Mormon prophet lay dead. The mob also killed Smith's brother Hyrum. Taylor fell grievously wounded while Richards escaped with only a superficial wound.[53] Religious intolerance had cut short the life of one of the most unusual and dynamic leaders in frontier history. As the people of Nauvoo began to mourn their beloved prophet, they had no inkling of the greater tragedies they would face in the years to come.[54]

CHAPTER 5

Mormon Colonies in Texas, 1845–58

Few in Nauvoo had ever anticipated the prophet's death. Apparently Joseph Smith himself did not foresee his own death in time to choose a clear successor. This oversight led to a problem that would shake the foundations of the city for the next two years. Who would replace Smith?

Smith organized the power structure of his religious and political kingdom in several independent tiers. In a manner similar to the separation of powers employed in the U.S. federal structure, each group had specific authority related to the governing of the church, while none had absolute power. The situation following Smith's death was comparable to the confusion that might occur if a U.S. president were to die in office without a clear line of succession. Without the guidance of the Constitution, the vice president might claim control, while the Senate, House, Cabinet, and Supreme Court might make similar assertions. This is the problem the Mormons faced as they tried to determine who, if anyone, could replace their beloved prophet.

In the aftermath members of the Quorum of the Twelve Apostles, under the leadership of Brigham Young, felt that they were in charge. Likewise Smith's personal counselors believed that they should be in charge.[1] Some members of the Council of Fifty felt that their organization was to take over affairs of the church. Smith's widow felt that his oldest son should succeed him. To make matters more confusing, other would-be prophets stepped forward to claim their place at the head of the church. This was the biggest challenge the struggling religion had ever faced.[2]

Since none of these groups was particularly concerned about Smith's Texas plan at that time, the four Texas commissioners remained unsure of how to proceed. On July 11, 1844, Woodworth wrote a letter to Houston that reflected the state of confusion in Nauvoo:

> The great excitement surround [sic] us has been sufficient apology for all seeming neglect, and I hope your excellency will favor me with a letter stating anything new which may have occurred & you shall hear from me again more positively when I get a letter.... Recent occurrences has [sic] prevented me making the propositions desired. If you still consider the plan practicable, communicate and a reply shall be forthcoming.[3]

No further communication is known to exist between Houston and the Mormons in Nauvoo. By the fall of 1844, the Mormons struggled for their very survival, while Texas concentrated on its annexation treaty with the United States. In the midst of these more pressing issues, the dream of the Mormon Kingdom of God in the Texas Republic faded into the background.

Back in Nauvoo, the power struggle continued. Young, now a commanding Mormon figure, garnered the most support. His argument that the Twelve Apostles should lead the church, just as after the death of Jesus Christ his apostles did the same, made sense to the majority of Mormons. The Quorum of the Twelve Apostles, under Young, was sustained as the ruling body of the church by a majority vote at a conference in August, 1844.[4] As head of the Twelve Apostles, it became clear that Young would eventually step forward as the next prophet of the church.

Recognizing Young's authority, those commissioners who were in charge of the Texas negotiations turned to their new leader for guidance. George Miller recalled that they planned to

> ... get the authorities together and clothe ourselves with the necessary papers, and proceed to meet the Texan Congress, as before Joseph's death agreed upon. Woodworth and myself waited on Brigham, requesting him to convene the authorities that the proper papers might be made out, so that we would be able to complete the unfinished negotiation of the treaty for the territory mentioned in my former letters. And to my utter astonishment, Brigham refused having anything to do in the matter; that he had no faith in it, and would do nothing

to raise means for our outfit or expenses. . . . I was really cast down and dejected.[5]

The *Journal History of the Church* also records the outcome of a later meeting in which Miller pled with Young to move to Texas: "Pres. Young informed Bishop Miller that his views were wild and visionary, that when the Saints moved hence, it would be to the Great Basin, where they would soon form a nucleus of strength and power sufficient to cope with mobs."[6] The four players in the Texas plan—Lyman Wight, George Miller, Lucien Woodworth, and Almon W. Babbitt—were puzzled by their new leader's response. Young had supported the Texas move just a short time before. On May 3, 1844, he was quoted as saying: "If any of the brethren wish to go to Texas we have no particular objection; you may send a hundred thousand there if you can in eighteen months."[7]

Much had changed in the few months since Young made that statement about Texas. Rumors abounded in Nauvoo that several men implicated in Smith's murder had fled to Texas. In the Republic they could potentially continue to make problems for the Latter-day Saints.[8] In addition the thought of serving as a military buffer between two warring nations could not have been appealing to the pragmatic Young. He wisely favored his predecessor's other plan of relocating to some remote corner of the far West where the Mormons would be isolated from the rest of the world.[9] Such a move demonstrated a siege mentality, but, based on Mormon experiences in Ohio, Missouri and Illinois, it was justified.

Wight clearly felt the deepest disappointment about the abandonment of the Texas negotiations. According to Wight, Smith had privately taken him aside in mid-April of 1844 and personally commissioned him to lead the church's entrance into Texas.[10] With characteristic zeal Wight believed that this was God's will for him in spite of what Young or any other so-called successor might say.[11] Initially Wight convinced Young to allow him to lead a group of volunteers to the Texas Republic.[12] Fearing that Wight could sway a large portion of the church to follow him, Young placed restrictions on his group. In a public meeting held on August 18, 1844, Young delivered a sermon in which he specified detailed instructions regarding Wight's Texas expedition:

There is no man who has any right to lead one soul out of this city by the consent of the Twelve, except Lyman Wight and George Miller, they have had the privilege of taking the "Pine Company" where they pleased, but not another soul has the consent of the Twelve to go with them ... and I tell you in the name of Jesus Christ that if Lyman Wight and George Miller take a course contrary to our counsel and not act in concert with us, they will be damned and go to destruction ... and I will destroy their influence in this Church with the help of God and my brethren.[13]

Clearly a power struggle had erupted between Young and Wight. As a fellow member of the Quorum of the Twelve, Wight saw himself as an equal to Young. Young's threats of damnation and destruction only widened the divide between the two stubborn men. Tensions quickly grew, and Wight could endure only one month in Nauvoo with Young before he decided to leave the city.[14] For some unknown reason George Miller decided not to follow Wight at this time. In spite of differences in feelings and personalities, Wight and his party left Nauvoo with the blessing of Young and the church. Wight remained an Apostle and his followers retained their church membership.[15]

In September, Wight led the 150 members of his Black River Lumber Company back to Wisconsin to settle affairs at the pinery and prepare for the move to Texas. After several more months in Wisconsin, Wight became anxious to leave for the Texas Republic and sold the pinery at a substantial loss. This was typical of the bad business practices that thwarted his ventures throughout his life.[16] On March 28, 1845, the Mormons of the Black River Lumber Company burned their homes and loaded boats headed south on the Mississippi River.[17]

On April 13, they landed upriver of Nauvoo at Duck Creek, Iowa, but chose not to join their fellow Mormons in the troubled city. While Wight did not explain this in his memoirs, it can be safely assumed that the tensions between him and Young prompted this decision.[18] Instead Wight's party settled for a short time near Davenport, Iowa, where they prepared for the long overland trek to the Texas Republic.[19]

Meanwhile Young prepared the main body of the church for their inevitable expulsion from Illinois. Young had no interest in Texas; rather he was drawn to Smith's other suggestions of Upper California, Oregon, or even the Rocky Mountains of northern Mexico. In 1842 Smith had prophesied

> ... the Saints would continue to suffer much affliction and would be driven to the Rocky Mountains, many would apostatize, others would be put to death by our persecutors or lose their lives in consequence of exposure or disease, and some of you will live to go and assist in making settlements and build cities and see the Saints become a mighty people in the midst of the Rocky Mountains.[20]

Like Wight, Young felt that he too needed to remain true to Smith's vision. Young felt that he could keep the idea of a Mormon nation alive in the remote West or Southwest.

Whether Wight had such lofty aspirations as he headed south for Texas is unknown. Most likely he envisioned a Mormon settlement similar to the community of Kirtland, Ohio, where his own religious life began.[21] In the Texas Republic he could return to the "common stock" economic system of Christian communalism practiced by the Campbellites and modified by the Mormons. It must be remembered that the Mormons of that era were people of considerable faith. Fifteen years of frequent moves and hardship made them rather hardened adventurers. Following the doctrines of his religion, Wight must have believed that God would bring good fortune to his Texas venture.[22]

Wight did not see himself as a spiritual successor to Smith. In fact he believed that Smith's son, Joseph Smith III, was eventually to lead the church. Wight claimed that while he was imprisoned with the elder Smith in Missouri, the prophet had appointed young Joseph III to replace him.[23] In 1844 Smith's son was only twelve years old and understandably shied away from his father's dangerous occupation.[24] Wight, no doubt, looked forward to the day when young Joseph would take his place at the head of the church.

In September, 1845, Wight's party of around 150 men, women, and children loaded up recently purchased wagons and teams, and began their fourteen-hundred-mile journey to the Texas Republic.[25] Slowly they crossed through Iowa, Missouri, Kansas, and Indian Territory. After six deaths and more than two months of travel, they crossed the Red River directly north of modern-day Dallas, on November 10, 1845.[26] Over the next week they pressed forward to an abandoned fort in Grayson County, called Georgetown. There they settled for the winter of 1845–46.[27]

This was a pivotal time in the Republic. Both the U.S. Congress and the Texas Congress had finally ratified the annexation treaty. All that remained was for President Polk to sign the Texas Admission Act into law. This signing took place on December 21, 1845, just weeks after the Mormons arrived.[28] A formal flag lowering and changing-of-the-guard ceremony took place on January 19, 1846, officially signaling the end of the Republic.[29] So the Mormon entrance into Texas corresponded closely to Texas annexation and statehood. Annexation and a Mormon settlement in Texas still seemed to support Smith's goals. Wight must have taken some satisfaction in witnessing the fulfillment of his mentor's dream.

Unbeknownst to Wight, while his small group wintered comfortably in the mild Texas weather, the main body of the church in Nauvoo was facing war once again. Systematic burnings of Mormon buildings as well as the murder and rape of several members of the church led to a resentful resignation in Nauvoo. Young met with Governor Ford and Senator Douglas in October, 1845, to discuss a peaceful resolution. During the negotiations they agreed that the Mormons would abandon the city in early spring of 1846. To ensure compliance, the Mormons were not allowed to plant crops.[30]

Within months the state government began harassing Young, and rumors circulated that Governor Ford had called for federal troops stationed in Missouri to destroy Nauvoo and all its Mormon inhabitants. Evidence suggests that the Governor circulated these rumors to coerce the Mormons out of the state earlier than planned. In all likelihood he had no intentions of their mass annihilation.[31]

Young did not want to take chances with the unsympathetic governor. Fearing terrible bloodshed, Young began the mass exodus from Illinois's largest city in the middle of winter. Thousands left their comfortable homes and crossed the frozen Mississippi to settle in primitive shelters in Iowa. By spring of 1846, Young emerged as the leader of some sixteen thousand impoverished Mormons living in camps spread across hundreds of miles.[32]

That same spring Wight led his group past the small village of Dallas and continued towards the state capital of Austin. The infrastructure of

Texas remained underdeveloped at the time, and the party had to traverse several rivers with their wagons and livestock. With some difficulty they reached the Austin area on June 6, 1846. Wight selected an area at the falls of the Colorado River about four miles north of town for his first settlement.[33] His selection proved ironic as this location marked the corner of the original territory that Woodworth offered to buy from Houston in April, 1844.[34]

The Mormons immediately began construction of a water mill. After several years in the milling business in Wisconsin, Wight's group of Mormons had gained two valuable skills—the building and operating of water-powered mills and the processing of lumber. These much-needed skills kept the Mormons safe in their new Texas home. The mill at Mormon Springs, as it came to be known, was the first grist mill in the region. After the Mormons' first public meeting in Austin, an old Texan observed that the townspeople felt that the Mormons "were a lawless band, and the subject of rising up and driving them from the country was strongly advocated." Once the Texans realized the benefit of the Mormon mill, however, they welcomed the newcomers to their community.[35] Soon the Mormons were grinding corn and constructing buildings for the residents of Austin. They even won the contract to build Austin's first jail.[36]

Their military experience presented another saving attribute for the Texas Mormons. "Colonel" Lyman Wight created quite a spectacle in Austin: he had pistols strapped to his hips and traveled with armed bodyguards.[37] With only 500 inhabitants in Austin, the 150 Mormons contributed greatly to the defense of the city. Because of renewed hostilities against Mexico and with Comanche raids still a threat, the citizens of Austin ignored "objectionable features" of Mormon doctrine and let the Mormons live in peace.[38]

In October, 1846, Mormon Springs inexplicably ran dry. Wight took this to be a sign from God and sent explorers south to find another suitable site for a mill and settlement. On November 14, the exploration party returned with good news. Just seventy-five miles to the south they found a suitable location on the Pedernales River, near the German colony of Fredericksburg in the Texas hill country. To secure permission to settle on the original Prussian land grant, Wight met with Baron Otfried Johannes von Meuesbach in New Braunfels. The baron, pleased to have skilled laborers and a mill nearby, deeded a tract of land to the Mormons along the river.[39]

The German colonists in Fredericksburg had suffered terrible hardship because of their difficult migration. The Mormons, in their new town, called Zodiac, expressed sympathy toward their benefactors. With their newly constructed mills, they ground grains, cut lumber, and made furniture, much of which went directly to Fredericksburg. The Germans greatly benefited from the services, and the Mormons benefited equally from the employment. Although very few Germans ever embraced the religion, the Mormons left a distinct stamp on Fredericksburg.[40] The Latter-day Saints influenced much of the early material culture, architecture, and agriculture of the town.[41]

Unknown to the Mormons of Zodiac, far to the north the winter and spring of 1847 brought great adversity to Young and his followers. Fifteen thousand Mormons joined the western trek across the Great Plains in emigrant parties escaping the United States and headed for northern Mexican territory. On July 24, 1847, the advance party rode into the valley of the Great Salt Lake. Young, sick with a fever that nearly took his life, propped himself up from a carriage and spoke the words that all had waited for: "This is the place whereon we will plant our feet and where the Lord's people will dwell."[42] Smith's dream of a theocratic Kingdom of God became a reality not in southern Texas, but in the Great Basin of northern Mexico.

Not all Mormons followed Young. Some followers of Smith's gospel chose to retain their identity as Mormons while refusing to acknowledge Young as their leader. Smith's first wife, Emma Hale Smith, for example, tenaciously remained in Illinois in the years following her husband's death.[43] In the aftermath of Young's exodus west, several hundred Mormons, following various leaders, remained dispersed throughout the Midwest.[44] Others became disillusioned with the hard trek across the continent with Young and dropped out along the way. George Miller disagreed with Young's leadership and parted ways with the main body of the church on the Great Plains. Remembering his own role in the Texas negotiations, Miller moved south to find Wight and the Black River Lumber Company of which he had once been part.[45]

Miller and his party eventually reached Zodiac on February 1, 1848. According to Miller, Zodiac already exuded prosperity: "The community had a grist and saw mill, which they had but six or nine months before my arrival got into full operation. They had also a turning lathe, blacksmith and wagon shop, together with comfortable houses.... Wight's company seemed to be in a prosperous condition."[46] Miller noted that the group languished under the debt of some two thousand dollars owed to the citizens of Austin and blamed Wight specifically for his poor business skills.[47] The Mormons of Zodiac had indeed returned to the "common stock" communal economic system practiced by Wight and the Campbellites of Kirtland, Ohio. As Miller noted, Wight's socialist system did not seem to be working to the financial advantage of the Mormons in Texas.

Lingering debt was not the only problem faced by the Mormons of Zodiac. Wight's notoriously hard drinking verged on alcoholism.[48] In addition he may have been developing an addiction to opiates contained in common patent medicines of the time. Both habits clouded his judgment and at times alienated him from his peers.[49] George Miller eventually had his fill of Wight and his style of leadership and left Zodiac an angry man in the fall of 1849. Miller ultimately joined another Mormon splinter group in Michigan. He eventually tired of them as well and died en route to California in the late 1850s.[50] In spite of defections the population of Zodiac remained stable and even grew over time.[51]

In 1848 Young sent church elders Preston Thomas and William Martindale to locate Wight and his people and bring them back to the Mormon theocratic state of Deseret.[52] Now established in the Rocky Mountains, Young wanted to reclaim those who had not followed him west. Young had hoped for a reconciliation with Wight, but the report of the elders shattered that hope. Among other complaints, accounts that Young had called him a coward for leaving Nauvoo had infuriated Wight.[53] Wight finished his interview with the elders by saying that "he would see them all damned to the lowest hell before he would do it."[54] Wight was officially disfellowshipped from the church in 1849 as a result.[55]

Young's interest in Texas extended beyond just Wight and his group. He saw Texas as fertile ground for conversion. He began sending missionaries to Texas by late 1847 or early 1848.[56] Apparently these missionaries had a degree of success in Texas.[57] The new converts, associated with the main church now headquartered in Utah Territory, had nothing to do with Wight's group. While these initial converts stayed in Texas, Young eventually encouraged them to join with the body of the church in the Utah Territory. Nearly one thousand Texas converts to Mormonism made the long journey to Utah before the Civil War.[58]

Despite the success of the Utah church, Wight would have nothing to do with it. Even Wight's old associate in the Texas negotiations, Woodworth, visited Zodiac to try to bring him back to the fold.[59] Little is known of this meeting except that it too ended in failure. Initially Wight's achievements seemed to validate his actions in settling in Texas. In early 1851 he received a large government contract for grinding corn. This could have secured the economic prosperity of Zodiac for years. Unfortunately Wight's victories proved short-lived. At the pinnacle of his success, the Pedernales River flooded and destroyed his mills. After four years of struggle Wight commanded his people to pull up stakes once again.[60]

Wight's scouts located suitable property on Hamiltons Creek, which they immediately purchased and named Hamilton Valley.[61] In the summer of 1851 the people of Zodiac abandoned their flood-drenched town and moved to the new mill site.[62] Besides their usual grist and saw mills, the Mormons also established a furniture factory in the new town. As farming languished in this area, the furniture factory became the financial savior of the settlement. Mormon craftsmen turned out thousands of chairs, baskets, and other pieces of furniture that they promptly sold throughout central Texas.[63]

The sale of furniture was insufficient to sustain the colony for long. The Mormons of Hamilton Valley could not duplicate the financial successes that they had enjoyed in Zodiac. Farming conditions were substandard, local timber proved to be of poor quality, and the Mormons failed to procure any government contracts.[64] Looking for a way out, Wight sold the mills to a wealthy local landowner.[65] After only two years in Hamilton Valley, not everyone welcomed Wight's wanderlust. At least three families decided to stay behind to work the mills for the new owner.[66]

The majority of Wight's company left Hamilton Valley without any clear idea of where they were going. After an unsuccessful attempt at prospecting in the Riley Mountains, in 1854 the group moved to a spot along the Medina River, near modern-day Bandera and what was then the western frontier of Texas settlement.[67] As usual they went to work immediately at building a mill. The Mormons in Bandera mainly manufactured shingles that they sold to surrounding settlements. Since other employment proved scarce, the shingle business emerged as the primary economic underpinning of the community.[68] The extra income also allowed them to set up a farm and build more permanent homes downstream at Mountain Valley.[69]

Although the local Anglo population welcomed the Mormons and their mill, the Comanches viewed them as easy targets. During the 1850s the U.S. Army indiscriminately attacked Native Americans on the Texas frontier, which provoked the wrath of even formerly peaceful tribes and initiated tough times for the Comanches.[70] The Mormon cattle and horses at Mountain Valley provided an easy source of food and income for the desperate and angry Native Americans. The Comanche depredations became so severe over the next four years that it almost bankrupted the settlement.[71] Still the little community persevered. Furniture making again became an essential part of the community. The Mormons were particularly well known throughout the region for their chairs and bedsteads, which they sold in central Texas.[72]

The years of living the unstable life of an early Mormon had taken their toll on Wight. He never seemed able to develop deep roots or feel completely at ease in any home. In addition Wight worried about the possibility of a civil war erupting in the United States.[73] On January 1, 1858, he prophesied of the danger such a war would bring and claimed that after twelve years it was time to leave Texas.[74] As the Mormons of Mountain Valley prepared to leave once again, dissension filled the ranks. Even one of Wight's sons, weary of the constant moves, initially refused to leave.[75] By spring Wight convinced most of the group of the necessity of moving north. On March 30, 1858, the Mormon wagons once again began rolling towards an unknown destination north of the Red River between Texas and Indian Territory.[76]

The years of hardship, including imprisonment and torture, also took their toll on the sixty-one-year-old Wight. On the first night of travel, just outside of San Antonio, Wight became ill with a fever. His pains drove him to take heavy doses of laudanum to ease his discomfort.[77] Wight, already addicted for years to the opium-based patent medicine, suffered a seizure. The combination of fever, dehydration,

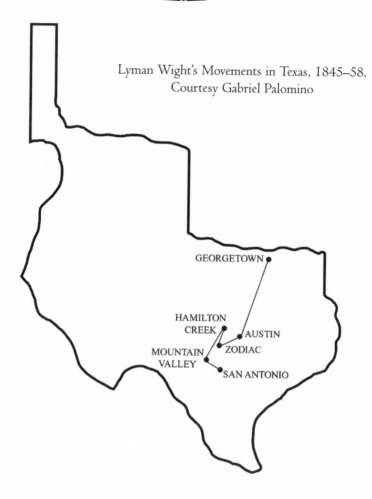

Lyman Wight's Movements in Texas, 1845–58.
Courtesy Gabriel Palomino

and opium killed him almost immediately. Shocked by their leader's death, the Mormons took his body back to their old home in Zodiac for burial.[78]

Without Wight's dynamic leadership, the Texas Mormon community soon collapsed. Some decided to try their luck back with the main body of the church in Utah. Others, anxious to accept Joseph Smith III as their new prophet, moved north to Iowa to join the Reorganized Church of Jesus Christ of Latter Day Saints. Some decided to remain in Texas. Within a generation these families lost all connection with Mormonism and assimilated into the mainstream of Texas society. After twelve years of struggle on the Texas frontier, the venture was over.[79]

CHAPTER 6

The Aftermath

Perhaps the greatest influence the Mormons had on Texas came as the result of their not relocating to the Nueces Strip. Sam Houston was never able to find colonists willing to settle the region. Without an Anglo population base along the Rio Grande, the Nueces Strip remained a problem for the Texas Republic. Around the time of Joseph Smith's assassination and the end of the Mormon negotiations, Mexico again declared war on Texas. Mexican general Woll stepped up operations around the Rio Bravo, and few Anglos dared cross the Nueces River into the disputed strip.[1]

The proposed annexation of Texas by the United States further provoked the wrath of Mexico. President James K. Polk offered to buy the Nueces Strip as a means to end the boundary dispute. Unfortunately he tied the deal into a greater purchase of the entire Southwest. This proved unacceptable to Mexico, which promptly ended all diplomatic relations with the United States.[2]

In July, 1845, President Polk sent troops under Gen. Zachary Taylor to Corpus Christi, at the northeastern end of the Nueces Strip, to monitor the situation. The forces remained in Corpus Christi for several months while the United States and Texas ratified the final treaty of annexation. Then in a controversial move to extend U.S. control over the Nueces Strip, Polk ordered Taylor south to the Rio Grande.[3] It is likely that this move was intended to provoke war with Mexico. To make the American presence clear, Taylor erected a fort directly across the river from the Mexican city of Matamoros in April, 1846. After several weeks of a relatively uneventful standoff, Mexican artillery fired on the American troops at the newly christened Fort Texas.[4] This action led to the Battles of Palo Alto and Resaca De Las Palmas, which ultimately initiated the U.S.–Mexican War.[5] The subsequent arrival of thousands of American soldiers and support personnel solidified U.S. political control of the territory and created a mixed Mexican-Anglo culture that exists in the Nueces Strip to this day.

The U.S.–Mexican War not only shaped the destiny of Texas, the United States, and Mexico, it also influenced the future of the Church of Jesus Christ of Latter-day Saints. The power vacuum created by the war allowed Young to establish and settle his State of Deseret in the Great Basin while unopposed by the Mexican government. The Treaty of Guadalupe-Hidalgo, which ended the war in 1848, put the Mormons in Deseret back under the jurisdiction of the United States. For the next decade the federal government and Young would be at odds.

This power struggle culminated in the Utah War of 1857–58, which threatened to displace the Mormons once again. This strange war resulted from rumors started by federal judicial appointees in the Utah Territory. The Nauvoo experience had sealed Mormon distrust of the U.S. court system. In compensation they devised their own system of ecclesiastical, civil, and criminal courts. The seemingly disreputable character of the federal appointees strengthened the resolve of the Mormons to stay aloof from the U.S. judicial system.[6]

This conflict came to a head in 1857, when a judge named W. W. Drummond relayed false reports to President James Buchanan that the Mormons were in rebellion against the United States.[7] Garland Hurt, a territorial Indian agent, further reported that the Mormons had joined forces with Native Americans to retake Utah from the United States.[8]

Without consulting independent sources the president amassed the largest peacetime army in American history up to that point and sent it west to suppress the Mormon uprising. Congress initially supported the war. Northern members of Congress wanted to make an example of Utah in order to discourage the secession of southern states. Southern members of Congress in turn desired to divert national attention away from the slavery issue.[9] Amid the rumors and cries for bloodshed, one old statesman called for restraint: Houston. At the end of his life and political career, Houston would have one final influence on the destiny of Smith's church.

An oral tradition persists among the Latter-day Saints about Houston's attitude toward them in the years just prior to the Utah War. Although some facts seem exaggerated, the basic story possesses a note of truth. In the account Smith's cousin and prominent member of the Council of Fifty, George A. Smith, traveled to Washington, D.C. to discuss business related to the territory. Upon arrival Smith immediately asked for a meeting with Senator Houston of Texas to discuss the matter. In the account both men became immediate and fast friends:

> The two old men then laid down on the floor with a pillow under their heads and laid on the back of chairs and went on talking.... After General Houston and President Smith had been talking a little while President Smith became cold ... whereupon General Houston got a parcel which he had and took a Navajo Blanket out of the parcel and put it over his shoulders and again went on talking.... General Houston was always a great friend to the West and remained a friend to the Mormon people up to the time of his death.[10]

Perhaps these senior politicians speculated about how different the history of the Republic might have been had things worked out differently back in 1844. Whatever actually occurred in this meeting probably helped reinforce Houston's attitude toward the Mormons and the impending Utah War.

In 1857 the Mormons met the federal challenge with a scorched-earth policy. They burned all grazing areas in the plains. Mormon-owned Fort Bridger and Fort Supply in Wyoming were also burned before they could fall into the hands of the army.[11] Mormon guerillas attacked military supply trains and destroyed more than three months' worth of provisions without killing a single U.S. soldier. The unexpected resistance forced the army to winter in the ruins of Fort Bridger.[12] While the army remained stalemated in Wyoming, Congress began to debate the practicality of the invasion. Houston led the most outspoken critics of the Utah war.[13]

While Houston believed that the Mormons needed to submit themselves to federal authority, he doubted they intended rebellion. He saw the war as a thinly veiled effort to build up a standing army of some size.[14] He adamantly persisted in his opinion that such a large army could

not conquer Utah, and he suggested that a volunteer force, already familiar with the Rocky Mountains, could better deal with the Mormon situation. In a characteristic use of levity to diffuse a tense situation, he suggested that volunteers might indeed like Utah and especially the Mormon
women. Their intermarriage with Mormons would then bring the whole
affair to a close without bloodshed.[15]

As far as charges that the Native Americans were collaborating with
the Mormons, he chastised Congress: "it has driven them to the Mormons; they are their allies. Why? Because they were killed when they
wanted peace. Because the Mormons have not committed a correspond-
ing wrong on them, they are the allies of the Mormons. They will always
go where friendship and justice are accorded to them."[16]

Houston, a great advocate for Native American rights, remained
impressed by the Mormons' treatment of their Native American
neighbors.

After several weeks Houston received correspondence from Utah that
changed the whole tone of his attack. The letter, from an unnamed Mormon, made him realize the war was not only unjust, but most likely un-
warranted as well. Again he addressed the Congress:

I received the other day from a very intelligent Mormon whom I
knew in Texas . . . a letter of seven pages. In that letter he takes a
comprehensive view of this subject. He protests most solemnly that
there never would have been the least hostility to the authorities of
the United States if the President had sent respectable men there. He
says that Governor Brigham Young has been anxious to get rid of the
cares of office, and would freely have surrendered it and acknowl-
edged the authority of the United States; but that men have gone
there, who have made threats that they would hang them, and even
threats of a character that renders them more sensitive in relation to
their families, and that they expect nothing but rapine and destruction to ensue . . . [17]

Indeed, that letter summed up the Mormon position in the Utah War.
The corrupt and insensitive federal appointees had backed the church
into a corner with threats of death and destruction. If the president
would send honest individuals to the territory, Young agreed to submit

to their authority. This letter proved correct later that year when Young adopted that very policy.

The author of this letter is unknown. Perhaps it was someone involved in the negotiations of 1844. Whoever it was, his letter turned Houston completely against any further hostilities against the Mormons. In those seven pages the author clearly described some of the defensive measures undertaken in the territory. Young and much of the leadership of the church went into hiding in the mountains, canyons, and smaller settlements outside of the capital.[18] Thousands of Mormon troops armed themselves with weapons carried in from Mormon settlements in California and Nevada. After seeing so many of their homes occupied repeatedly by their enemies, the Mormons vowed to burn their cities rather than let them fall into enemy hands again.[19] Houston knew the army faced a bloodbath.

Senator Houston tried to convey the foolishness of the venture to Congress by comparing the imminent battle to the crushing defeat of Napoléon at Moscow:

> They will find Salt Lake, if they ever reach it, a heap of ashes. . . . Just as sure as we are now standing in the Senate, these people, if they fight at all, will fight desperately. They are defending their homes. They are fighting to prevent the execution of threats that have been made, which touch their hearths and their families; and depend upon it they will fight until every man perishes before he surrenders. . . . I say your men will never return, but their bones will whiten the valley of Salt Lake. If war begins, the very moment one single drop of blood is drawn, it will be the signal of extermination.[20]

Houston further chastised the government and military for not responding to Young's obvious attempts at a peace settlement.[21] Apparently his words elicited support. Public opinion turned against the president, and the Utah War became known as "Buchanan's Blunder." More than five thousand troops huddled starving and freezing on the plains, waiting to fight a war against thirty thousand Mormons and their army. Young, perhaps for the only time in his life, enjoyed a certain folk- hero status in the eastern press. In an attempt to salvage some dignity from the fiasco,

Buchanan offered a full pardon to the Mormons on April 6, 1858, seven days after Lyman Wight had died in Texas.[22]

The negotiated peace required that Young step down as governor. The Mormons allowed the invading force to march through the Great Salt Lake City on the condition that they not occupy the city. They were to keep marching to a bivouac point forty miles away. To ensure that the army would honor its promise, members of the reinstituted Nauvoo Legion filled the buildings of the city with hay and stood ready to apply the torch if the army dared stop within city limits. Ironically the man leading the U.S. forces through the city was Col. Albert Sidney Johnston, a former secretary of war of the Texas Republic under Houston. With equal irony the United States would brand Johnston himself a rebel when he took a commission in the Confederate States Army only three years hence.[23]

The first week of April, 1858, ended an era in Texas-Mormon relations. With Wight's death it signaled the end of Smith's Kingdom of God in Texas. With the help of Houston, this week also ushered in a new era in Mormon relations with the United States. So as one dream died, a new vision was born: an American nation that could tolerate and eventually embrace the Church of Jesus Christ of Latter-day Saints.

The integration of Mormons into mainstream American society proved a painful process that required decades of conflict. This struggle challenged the notion of religious freedom in the United States well into the twentieth century. To survive, the Mormons were forced to see themselves in a new light and even to re-create themselves as model citizens. As the twentieth century wore on, the Latter-day Saints no longer persisted in being a society unto themselves, but rather became another facet of the diverse American cultural mosaic.

The church, perhaps unwittingly, also contributed to the rise of the modern United States. Smith had originally planned to change the world through his political Kingdom of God. In the violent aftermath of that failure, his successor, Young, created a system of colonization that ensured American domination of the West and Southwest.

Aside from the Mormon role in America's manifest destiny, the church continues to make a mark on American culture and history. Eventually protected by the same federal government that originally sought to suppress it, the Church of Jesus Christ of Latter-day Saints has grown well beyond the expectations of the nation. The close of the twentieth century saw church membership surpass ten million.[24] While history has yet to write the final chapter on the Church of Jesus Christ of Latter-day Saints, the imprint that the church's history has made on the United States is indelible. In the end it is perhaps this shared influence that remains the greatest legacy of the Texas-Mormon experience.

CHAPTER 7

Conclusion

The 1844 negotiations between the Texas Republic and the Church of Jesus Christ of Latter-day Saints resulted from the need for security and self-rule on the western frontier. While the negotiations may seem naively ambitious by modern standards, in the context of both Texas and Mormon history, they offered a possible solution to both groups' problems.

From the organization of their church in 1830, Mormons suffered abuse from their intolerant neighbors. When the persecution turned violent, as it did in Ohio, Missouri, and Illinois, the Mormons began a search for a new homeland. The unique teachings of the religion's founder, Joseph Smith, convinced church members that they were capable, if not obligated, to form a theocratic nation to help usher in the second coming of Jesus Christ and the millennium. Smith called this theocratic nation the Kingdom of God and appointed himself a king. He also organized a Council of Fifty to govern the temporal affairs of the kingdom.

The Texas Republic experienced its own share of difficulties during this time. The war of independence with Mexico left a disputed border between the nations. The Republic's policies toward Native Americans provoked frequent attacks by the Comanches on the western frontier. Poor fiscal policy during the late 1830s led to the overprinting of paper money and devaluation of the currency of Texas. President Houston vowed in 1841 that he would find ways to manage these three problems.

Houston's obvious solution was to have the Republic annexed by the United States. Unfortunately for Houston, the debate over the slavery issue stalled any immediate annexation plans by the United States. Houston entertained other options, including settling foreign colonists along the western and southern frontier. The sale of public lands would bring in much needed cash, while the colonists themselves would provide a buffer for attacks by Mexicans and Native Americans.

Smith also considered his options for security. After being driven from homes in New York, Ohio, and Missouri, the Mormons built a large city called Nauvoo on the banks of the Mississippi River. By 1844 armed mobs motivated by lust for Mormon property and religious intolerance began attempting to drive the Mormons from their Illinois homes. To provide for his defense, Smith formulated several plans. First, Smith announced his candidacy for U.S. president. As chief executive he could ensure fair treatment for his followers. If that failed, Smith asked Congress for permission to raise a large volunteer army to police the frontier between Texas and the Oregon Territory. With Nauvoo as the headquarters for such an army, no mob would dare attack. Smith's third and most radical plan dealt with removing the church further into the frontier. Options for a new homeland included Oregon, Upper California, and the Texas Republic.

As 1844 wore on, Smith's plans failed one by one. Congress would not seriously consider either Smith's presidential candidacy or volunteer army. His preliminary inquiry into Oregon revealed that many anti-Mormons from Missouri had already settled in that land. Texas, on the other hand, seemed more promising. Both the secular and religious newspapers of Nauvoo had taken an interest in Texas affairs for several years. Smith built a presidential platform, based in part, on Texas annexation. In addition Smith received letters from one of his Twelve Apostles, pushing for immigration to the Republic.

In the spring of 1844, Smith sent Lucien Woodworth as an ambassador to meet with Houston in Austin. Woodworth carried instructions to purchase the sparsely populated western and southern regions of the Republic. Houston refused to sell such a large tract of land. Realizing that the five-thousand-member Mormon army might make a formidable barrier in the south, Houston offered to sell Woodworth the disputed Nueces Strip. Woodworth returned to Nauvoo in May with the good news. Smith called three commissioners to make a treaty with the Texas Congress during the coming fall.

The following month Smith wavered in his resolve to establish his own nation. He even began meeting with a private Texas land speculator to purchase a smaller tract of land. Whatever his plans, Smith's hopes for an independent Mormon homeland in the Texas-Mexico borderlands collapsed when an Illinois mob brutally took his life. In the resulting power struggle, the Texas negotiations faded into the background. Brigham Young eventually emerged as the new leader of the Church of Jesus Christ of Latter-day Saints. When the three commissioners from the Texas negotiations approached Young about returning to meet with Houston, Young would have nothing to do with the plan.

Lyman Wight, another of Smith's Twelve Apostles, could not accept Young's decision on the Texas matter. According to Wight, Smith personally commissioned him to lead the first party to Texas after the negotiations were completed. Wight intended to fulfill that charge despite anyone's opinion. In 1845 Wight began his journey to the Texas Republic accompanied by 150 men, women, and children. Wight and his group started settlements in five Texas counties. While the group experienced some success as millers and carpenters, they eventually became estranged from the main body of the church that was then living in Utah. When Wight died in 1858, the group dispersed throughout the United States.

Although no permanent Mormon settlements survived in Texas, the Mormon association with the Republic proved beneficial. In 1857 President James Buchanan sent an army of five thousand to the Utah Territory to crush an alleged rebellion by the Mormons. Senator Houston of Texas openly denounced this otherwise popular campaign. With the help of Houston's impassioned speeches, public opinion turned. President Buchanan eventually offered pardons to the Mormons, effectively ending the Utah War.

In the long term both Texas and the Mormons benefited from the negotiations of 1844. Although the parties never signed a treaty, Mormons still immigrated to the Republic. Wight's Mormon colonists helped many fledgling communities in Texas through their milling and carpentry skills. Perhaps the greater influence demonstrated itself in Houston's sympathetic attitude toward the church. Through his help the Mormons survived the Utah War and assimilated into mainstream American culture. The resulting Mormon colonization of the American West and Southwest then, in turn, ensured the American goal of manifest destiny.

Mormon Terminology

Any student of a distinct cultural group knows that there is often a vocabulary that one must learn. In spite of the assimilation of twentieth-century church members, the Mormons of the nineteenth century were a distinct and isolated group. This isolation has resulted in an entire lexicon of Mormonism. The following terms are clarified to assist the first-time reader of Mormon history:

The Book of Mormon: In 1820 Joseph Smith had the first in a series of reported visions. These experiences eventually led him to a place near his home in Upstate New York, where he found a record, engraved upon plates of gold, of the ancient inhabitants of the Americas. Smith claimed that God gave him the ability to translate this record from a hybrid language of Egyptian and Hebrew. In 1830 he published the translation as the Book of Mormon. Called by critics "the Gold Bible," or "the Mormon Bible," the Book of Mormon is quite different from the Christian Bible as it centers on events on the American continents mainly between 600 B.C.E. and 400 C.E. The book is named for one of several American prophets credited with the actual writing of the book.

Church of Jesus Christ of Latter-day Saints: The official name of the Mormon church after 1838. Before that time it was known as the Church of Christ and the Church of the Latter-day Saints. The most common name for the church in the nineteenth century was the Mormon church.

Gentile: Mormons have historically used this term in the same context as Jews. To a Mormon, a Gentile is any non-Mormon, including unconverted Jews.

Lamanite: A term in the Book of Mormon to describe the ancestors of Native Americans. In common Mormon usage it also refers to anyone of either indigenous American or Polynesian descent. Considered by the church to be a blessed people in the last days, "Lamanites" compose nearly half the current church membership.

Mormon: Initially a pejorative term used for members of the Church of Jesus Christ of Latter-day Saints, but adopted early on by members to describe both themselves and their church. Members of the church also call themselves "Saints," used in the archaic Christian sense of the word, or "Latter-day Saints." All terms are used interchangeably in this book.

The Prophet: In Mormon usage the word refers to the leader of the church. Since the time of Joseph Smith, Mormons have affectionately called their current leader the prophet. This term is used in this book to refer to Joseph Smith.

The Temple: Temple worship has been an important part of Mormon theology since its early days. Inspired by rituals from a variety of sources, the temple is a place for advanced education and initiation for the most devout of church members. For the purposes of this book, the temple refers only to the Nauvoo temple that was under construction during the entire Nauvoo period of the church. The temple was the most important building in Nauvoo, and no expense was spared in its construction.

Articles about Texas in Nauvoo Newspapers, 1842–44

The following are excerpts from or summaries of articles that, although published in Nauvoo newspapers, originated in Texas and eastern newspapers. They show the type of exposure Mormons had to Texas from 1842 to 1844.

Wasp—William Smith (editor), Nauvoo, Illinois, 1842–43.

APRIL 16, 1842 (VOL. I, NO. 1)

The issue includes a reprint of Houston's letter describing the pillaging of San Antonio. "War shall now be waged against Mexico, nor will we lay aside our arms until we have secured the recognition of our Independence. Until then I will never rest satisfied, nor will the people of Texas. We invoke the God of Armies."

MAY 14, 1842 (VOL. I, NO. 5)

Houston writes to Santa Anna "You threaten to conquer Texas—we will war with Mexico. Your prentensions with ours you have refered [*sic*] to the social world and to the God of battles—we refer our cause to the same tribunals. The issue involves the fate of nations—destiny must determine—its course is only known to the tribunals of heaven ... our incentives will not be a love of conquest—it will be to disarm tyranny of its power."

JUNE 26, 1842 (VOL. I, NO. 11)

Santa Anna forces compulsory loans from the Catholic church. There is a description of war in the Yucatan. A Texas prisoner from Santa Fe escapes to San Antonio.

SEPTEMBER 3, 1842 (VOL. I, NO. 20)

Texas Congress declares war on Mexico, but Houston vetoes the action. Four hundred thousand acres of Cherokee lands will be sold for the benefit of Texas credit.

OCTOBER 8, 1842 (VOL. I, NO. 25)

The first of two articles that issue reports of seven thousand Mexican troops on the Texas frontier. The second says that Mexico is preparing to take back Texas. It laments the burdens put on the Mexican population by the mobilization. There was a fight in Texas during which fifty Mexican spies cowardly ran from a small band of Texans.

OCTOBER 29, 1842 (VOL. I, NO. 28)

Texas and Mexico are at war. Mexico clearly has the advantage. San Antonio is occupied and prominent citizens captured. Houston vows retribution.

NOVEMBER 12, 1842 (VOL. I, NO. 30)

Headline reads: "HIGHLY IMPORTANT FROM MEXICO—WAR AGAINST TEXAS—HER CONQUEST ALMOST CERTAIN." The article states that Santa Anna and the British are allied against Texas and that Texas will fall.

DECEMBER 3, 1842 (VOL. I, NO. 31)

The article outlines the atrocities of Mexican general Woll in San Antonio. Texans give him a good fight. There are rumors of Austin being burned. Woll executes a "noble hearted young Van Ness." "Is there not retributive justice for such acts of unmitigated cruelty?"

JANUARY 7, 1843 (VOL. I, NO. 36)

Santa Anna has goals of conquering the Yucatan and Texas and setting himself up as dictator. Texas is turning the war around in its favor. Mexico will not accept U.S. mediation.

FEBRUARY 22, 1843 (VOL. I, NO. 43)

Texas prisoners moved to Perote and forced to clean the streets. Santa Anna does away with the last of the federal system. Texans conquer Laredo and Monterrey. Van Ness is not shot after all, but rather sentenced to ten years prison. A second article says that Texas is running out of money and credit.

MARCH 1, 1843 (VOL. I, NO. 44)

Texas navy prepares to defend Galveston. An accident at a Catholic church in Texas kills twenty-eight.

MARCH 8, 1843 (VOL. I, NO. 45)

Texian army captured at Mier near Matamoros. It is feared they will be poorly treated although they are fine at the moment. The battle was very one-sided in favor of the Texian forces but they ran out of ammunition. The article praises both Texian skill and Mexican bravery.

MARCH 15, 1843 (VOL. I, NO. 46)

There has been bad flooding that has killed people and cattle. There are also confused and conflicting reports coming out of Texas in regard to the war.

APRIL 19, 1843 (VOL. I, NO. 51), LAST ISSUE OF THE WASP

Two Perote prisoners are released, which is a sign that Santa Anna is interested in peace. There are hopes that the remaining Perote prisoners will be released soon. A second article claims that Texians are organizing an invading army to cross at Del Rio to liberate the Perote prisoners.

Nauvoo Neighbor—John Taylor (editor), Nauvoo, Illinois, 1843–46.

MAY 10, 1843 (VOL. I, NO. 2)

Santa Anna sends an emissary to Washington, D.C., for help in ending war with Texas. Texas is promised statehood in Mexico with unprecedented independence and powers.

MAY 24, 1843 (VOL. I, NO. 4)

Houston is trying to stop Commodore Moore, a renegade in his navy, from attacking Campeche. A second article says that because of financial problems, Texas is considering annexation to Great Britain or becoming a free state in the United States in order to get northern investment. A third article reports that Mexico is forcing loans from the people. A fourth article claims that the Mexican navy confiscated a U.S. merchant ship and cargo.

JUNE 7, 1843 (VOL. I, NO. 6)

This article gives many details of the naval battle between Texas and Mexico in the southern Gulf of Mexico. Texas, under the renegade Moore, has a slight advantage, although little has resulted from it all.

JUNE 28, 1843 (VOL. I, NO. 9)

There are more details on Moore's naval battle in Mexico as well as a casualty list.

JULY 19, 1843 (VOL. I, NO. 12)

There is a large article about the armistice between Texas and Mexico.

AUGUST 16, 1843 (VOL. I, NO. 16)

Contains a report of one hundred Texan soldiers who skirmished with Mexican troops and were captured by the U.S. Army on American soil. Although some are credited with being intelligent, the general character of the Texan soldier was that of a marauder looking to take advantage of the Mexican. The troops were disarmed and escorted back to Texas.

SEPTEMBER 6, 1843 (VOL. I, NO. 19)

A Bexar prisoner describes the condition of the Perote prison. He claims treatment is good for the prisoners.

NOVEMBER 15, 1843 (VOL. I, NO. 29)

An English diplomat storms out of a ball in the Presidential Palace in Mexico because he sees the British flag (taken from Texans) hanging as a war trophy. Santa Anna closes all foreign commerce in Taos and Paso del Norte.

DECEMBER 6, 1843 (VOL. I, NO. 32)

Houston is rumored to be negotiating with Great Britain for annexation as a British province. Slavery would be outlawed and slave owners compensated. British relations with Mexico are worsening. The author views these negotiations as traitorous and dangerous to the United States.

DECEMBER 20, 1843 (VOL. I, NO. 34)

This is a repeat of the December 6, 1843, article with additional information claiming that Houston was going to allow a Mexican naval occupation of Galveston. This way he would have an excuse for allowing the British into Texas as liberators, which would convince the Texas people to accept annexation to Great Britain. Moore's naval actions in May, opposed by Houston, were actually designed to stop Houston from doing this. Moore should now be seen as a hero.

JANUARY 10, 1844 (VOL. I, NO. 37)

This issue carries a reprint of a letter from New Orleans. An unnamed Texan claims that the article from three weeks earlier is false. Houston is vindicated and sends a delegation to the Mexican capital to negotiate another armistice. Moore blamed for delaying peace by his actions. Houston is as popular as George Washington. Texas is thriving: "The cotton crop in Texas this season will be very large; and the corn crop is the largest we have ever had. Corn can be bought by the quantity at 20 cents per bushel; pork at $1.50 per cwt.; and, in fact, every kind of produce is very cheap and abundant, which is encouraging to emigrants,—We expect a large emigration this fall and winter. The health of Houston has been very good this summer. Our city is still improving. One or two large brick stores are going up, besides some wooden houses."

JANUARY 17, 1844 (VOL. I, NO. 38)

An article reprinted from the *Texas Telegraph* reports on the strange and marvelous Native American ruins found in the land. These ruins include ruined "castles or temples." A Mormon editorial claims this is proof of the authenticity of the Book of Mormon.

FEBRUARY 7, 1844 (VOL. I, NO. 41)

A front-page article compiled from two Texas papers (Houston and Galveston) reports on favorable conditions to be found in Texas. Trade is great and immigrants are thriving. Includes as proof the story of a German colony whose founders came destitute to Texas and are now flourishing ten years later in Austin and on the Colorado River: "Most of them brought nothing to the country with them, but their families; all their means being exhausted by their arrival. But they still retained a fund which nothing, save disease and bodily infirmity could render unavailable—their industry, skill and energy—their moral feelings, habits and common sense—all the funds necessary to acquire everything in Texas."

FEBRUARY 14, 1844 (VOL. I, NO. 42)

This is an extract from a talk Houston gave on Native American relations. He tells the sad story of a group of traders who in 1838 spoiled relations with the Comanches by poisoning a village and killing or injuring 350 men. The Comanches blamed all whites for the action, which Houston laments.

FEBRUARY 28, 1844 (VOL. I, NO. 44)

This article tells the story of Jim Bowie and his knife. He is seen as a bit of a rogue who invented a formidable weapon.

MARCH 6, 1844 (VOL. I, NO. 45)

A front-page article claims that Americans have been expelled from California. Ships from many nations are off Mexican shores. Texan prisoners in Perote are being abused. They are chained together and are dying from disease. Santa Anna is raising an army concentrated in Vera Cruz. Another article in same issue gives further details of the conditions of the Perote prisoners. They are almost naked, chained together, poorly fed, and given horrible medical treatment. The New Orleans–based author appeals to the Anglo-Saxon world to deplore this outrage. He mentions that the British have tried unsuccessfully to negotiate for their freedom or better treatment. The Texians are treated worse than the most notorious Mexican villain.

MARCH 13, 1844 (VOL. I, NO. 46)

A reprint from the *Houston Telegraph* celebrates the possibility of annexation, which cannot happen just yet because the U.S. Congress has adjourned for the session. The author claims that Houston has broad secret powers to accept annexation: "for our Congress, in secret session, has fully authorized the President to ratify the Treaty on the part of Texas."

The author expresses falsely optimistic excitement: "Ere another harvest is gathered in Texas, the broad banner of Washington may be unfurled in glory on our western border, and the burnished arms of American troops will be reflected from the sparkling waters of the Nueces. Westward! The star of empire takes its way!"

MARCH 20, 1844 (VOL. I, NO. 47)

This issue contains a front-page retraction of the past week's story. Annexation is a hoax. Many Texans actually don't want to be annexed. Texans won't consider annexation until they have tried further negotiations with Mexico for peace. There is more mention of British interests in Texas.

MARCH 27, 1844 (VOL. I, NO. 48)

There is a front-page reprint of the joint resolution sent to the Texas Congress from the U.S. Congress explaining terms for annexation.

APRIL 10, 1844 (VOL. I, NO. 50)

Directly under an advertisement: "For President GEN. JOSEPH SMITH, Nauvoo, Illinois" is an editorial stating that Texas annexation and Oregon Territory will dominate the presidential elections. Joseph Smith is correct in favoring annexation since the British will otherwise have the advantage if war breaks out with the United States over the Oregon dispute. Taken from another newspaper, a letter from Andrew Jackson states, "Remember, also, that if annexed to the United States, our western boundary would be the Rio Grande, which is of itself a fortification on account of its extensive, barren and uninhabitable plains. With such a barrier on our west we are invincible. The whole European world could not in combination against us, make an impression upon our Union. [New paragraph] From the Rio Grande, over land, a large army could not march, or be supplied, unless from the Gulf by water, which by vigilance, could always be intercepted; and to march an army near the gulf they could be harassed by militia, and detained till an organized force could be raised to meet them." There are also three stories dealing with annexation. This upstages coverage of the Mormon Semi-Annual Conference held the week prior. One pro-British annexation article states, "Those who are familiar with the hereditary obstinacy of the Spanish character must be satisfied that Mexico will never acknowledge the independence of Texas, unless forced to do so by threats from England."

MAY 29, 1844 (VOL. 2, NO. 7)
Included in this issue are several front-page articles and letters from different newspapers debating the annexation issue from several perspectives.

JUNE 5, 1844 (VOL. 2, NO. 8)
Mexico releases the last prisoner from Mier. The United States, Great Britain, and France are angry about Mexico's trade policies. France threatens war with Mexico. The annexation of Texas is anticipated by the United States.

JUNE 12, 1844 (VOL. 2, NO. 9)
A front-page article states that the population of Texas is two million (most likely a misprint), including twenty-five thousand slaves.

JUNE 19, 1844 (VOL. 2, NO. 10)
There is an editorial criticizing Mexico for threatening war against the United States if Texas is annexed.

JUNE 26, 1844 (VOL. 2, NO. 11)
The date given on the newspaper is June 19, obviously in error since that is issue no. 10's date. It was no doubt a bad week since the editor is imprisoned with Smith during this time. There is a front-page message from President Tyler in relation to the annexation of Texas. In addition there is an article about Sonoran bandits butchering Mexican militia in Sonora. They hang their body parts in trees. "Navahoe" beaten severely in New Mexico and many horses and cattle are taken from them. Mexican officials deny rumors that Texas has been annexed. Americans are thrilled at the possibility of annexation. Another pro-British article claims that Texas will not accept annexation and will remain forever tied to kindred England. There is great opportunity for employment in Texas.

JULY 3, 1844 (VOL. 2, NO. 12)
Joseph Smith is killed. The newspaper's editor, John Taylor, is gravely wounded. The British are shocked by rumors that Texas and the United

States have signed an annexation treaty and that only the Senate stands in the way of this happening. There is speculation that the Senate will not ratify.

JULY 10, 1844 (VOL. 2, NO. 13)

The annexation treaty is rejected by the Senate. President Tyler writes a long rebuttal. Another article states that France is against annexation since it would perpetuate slavery.

JULY 17, 1844 (VOL. 2, NO. 14)

Seventy miles northwest of Corpus Christi, Texas, a group of Mexican traders fight with Mexican troops trying to prevent smuggling into Mexico. The traders win the fight. Mexico offers commissions to all men willing to patrol the border and claims volunteers may keep all goods that they confiscate.

JULY 24, 1844 (VOL. 2, NO. 15)

Mexican government issues an edict giving the government broad powers to regain Texas.

AUGUST 21, 1844 (VOL. 2, NO. 17)

A letter from the *Galveston News* lays out the Mexican strategy for the reconquest of Texas. Santa Anna prepares for an invasion of Texas. Any Mexican found north of the Rio Bravo will be considered a traitor. All Texans are to be treated as traitors as well.

SEPTEMBER 11, 1844 (VOL. 2, NO. 20)

Many settlers in Texas are dying from disease. Another editorial claims that Santa Anna will be terribly defeated if he tries to invade Texas. The writer scoffs at rumors of an army of thirty thousand located outside San Luis Potosi. He takes a sympathetic view toward the ordinary Mexican conscript who will be forced to fight under deplorable conditions.

SEPTEMBER 18, 1844 (VOL. 2, NO. 21)

Mexico has sent a dispatch to Queen Victoria, and it is speculated that an invasion of Texas will not happen until after the dispatch has been answered by the queen.

OCTOBER 2, 1844 (VOL. 2, NO. 23)

Groups of Anglo desperadoes are fighting it out in Texas. Eighty have died so far and Houston refuses to intercede. The article also describes the bloody duel of two adversaries.

OCTOBER 9, 1844 (VOL. 2, NO. 24)

Houston intervenes to end the violence in East Texas, but murders still occur.

OCTOBER 23, 1844 (VOL. 2, NO. 26)

Two editorials argue opposite sides of the Texas Revolution. One claims that Mexico was extremely generous and that the Texans took advantage of the system. The other extols the greatness of Texas since the Revolution. A third article reports from Havana that Santa Anna received congressional support for his invasion of Texas. Houston is rumored to be asking for peace in exchange for concessions to Santa Anna.

NOVEMBER 13, 1844 (VOL. 2, NO. 29)

The last Perote prisoners are released. Santa Anna and his generals prepare for war with Texas. Woll and Houston do battle of words through the press.

DECEMBER 4, 1844 (VOL. 2, NO. 31)

A front-page article reports that Native Americans from the United States have attacked Texas at the Louisiana border.

DECEMBER 18, 1844 (VOL. 2, NO. 33)

Many immigrants are headed to Texas, although many are returning: "The latter complaining bitterly of the privations they had undergone."

Notes

CHAPTER I

1. Commonly called the Mormon church by those outside the faith. See Appendix A for a list of Mormon terminology.

2. Randolph P. Campbell, *Sam Houston and the American Southwest*, Library of American Biography, p. 93.

3. Joseph Smith, Jr., *History of the Church of Jesus Christ of Latter-day Saints*, vol. 4, pp. 479–80.

4. Members of the contemporary church largely prefer to be called Latter-day Saints. Members of the nineteenth-century church used both names. Given the period covered in this book, both names are used interchangeably.

5. The authoritative popular history of the Mormons is Leonard J. Arrington and Davis Bitton, *The Mormon Experience: The History of the Latter-day Saints.*

6. Campbell, p. 34.

7. In addition to the Campbell work, other important Houston biographies bear mention: Marshall De Bruhl, *Sword of San Jacinto: A Life of Sam Houston;* John Hoyt Williams, *Sam Houston: A Biography of the Father of Texas;* Llerena B. Friend, *Sam Houston: The Great Designer;* and Marquis James, *The Raven: A Biography of Sam Houston.* Also significant is Sam Houston, *The Autobiography of Sam Houston.*

8. John Edward Weems, *Dream of Empire: A Human History of the Republic of Texas, 1836–1846*, pp. 1–54.

9. Two treaties were actually made: a public treaty that called for the removal of Mexican troops south of the Rio Grande and a private treaty that established the Rio Grande as the border of Texas. See De Bruhl, p. 216, and also Matt S. Meier and Feliciano Rivera, *Dictionary of Mexican-American History*, p. 363.

10. The most exhaustive study of the Texas frontier before annexation can

be found in Joseph Milton Nance's two-volume study, *After San Jacinto: The Texas-Mexican Frontier, 1836–1841* and *Attack and Counterattack: The Texas-Mexican Frontier, 1842*. The Mexican view of Santa Anna's attempts to reclaim Texas during the Republic period can be found in Gen. Manuel A. Sanchez Lamego, *The Second Mexican-Texas War, 1841–1843*.

11. Campbell, p. 75.

12. For American views of manifest destiny and Texas annexation see Frederick Merk, *Manifest Destiny and Mission in American History: A Reinterpretation;* Norman A. Graebner, ed. *Manifest Destiny;* Norman E. Totorow, *Texas Annexation and the Mexican War: A Political Study of the Old Northwest;* and Robert W. Johannsen et al., *Manifest Destiny and Empire: American Antebellum Expansion.*

13. For details of the diplomatic issues related to Texas annexation see: David M. Pletcher, "The Annexation of Texas, 1843–1845," in *The Diplomacy of Annexation: Texas, Oregon, and the Mexican War,* pp. 113–226.

14. Campbell, p. 84. The first term of the Texas president was to be only two years, from December, 1836, to December, 1838. After that the subsequent presidents would serve a normal four-year term.

15. Meier and Rivera, p. 363.

16. *Anglo* was, and remains, the common term for Caucasians in Texas and is used in the Texas context in this book to describe those of northwestern European origin or descent. Outside of the Texas context the term *Euro-American* is used to describe this group.

17. Sue Flanahan, *Sam Houston's Texas,* pp. 10–11.

18. An exhaustive study of Texas frontier outposts during the Republic period can be found in Gerald S. Pierce, *Texas under Arms: The Camps, Posts, Forts, and Military Towns of the Republic of Texas, 1836–1846.*

19. Lamar was the vice president of the Republic under Houston.

20. Campbell, pp. 83–84.

21. For a detailed account of the Comanche raids on Texas see Donaly E. Brice, *The Great Comanche Raid: Boldest Indian Attack on the Texas Republic.*

22. Mexicans call the Rio Grande the Rio Bravo. In this book the river is called by both names depending on the perspective of the subject.

23. Lamego, pp. 2–7. The Lamego text is an invaluable source, as it relates the facts of these various campaigns from a Mexican perspective. See also Ángela Moyano Pahissa, *México y Estados Unidos: Orígines de una relación, 1819–1861,* and Gene M. Brack, *Mexico Views Manifest Destiny, 1821–1846: An Essay on the Origins of the Mexican War.*

24. Nance, *After San Jacinto,* pp. 252–315. Also see Milton Lindheim, *The Republic of the Rio Grande: Texans in Mexico, 1839–1840.*

25. Lindheim, pp. 16–17.

26. Lamego, pp. 53–62.

27. Works treating the colonial movement in Texas include William Campbell Binkley, *The Expansionist Movement in Texas, 1836–1850*; Rudolph Leopold Biesele, *The History of the German Settlements in Texas, 1831–1861*; Bobby Weaver, *Castro's Colony: Empresario Development in Texas, 1842–1865*; and Patrick L. O'Neill, "The Settling of Fisher and Miller's Colony in West Central Texas."

28. Seymour V. Conner, "Texas Land Policy," in *The Peters Colony of Texas*, pp. 7–18.

29. Ibid., pp. 16–17.

30. Ibid., "The Law of February 4, 1841," pp. 19–23.

31. Ibid., pp. 19–23.

32. Don H. Biggers, *German Pioneers in Texas: A Brief History of Their Hardships, Struggles and Achievements*, p. 18.

33. Binkley, pp. 99–101.

34. Ibid., p. 102.

35. The definitive source on life in Nauvoo is Robert Bruce Flanders, *Nauvoo: Kingdom on the Mississippi*.

CHAPTER 2

1. Smith, *History of the Church*, vol. 1, pp. 3–16.

2. Smith renamed the church as the Church of Jesus Christ of Latter-day Saints in 1838.

3. Kirtland is now a part of Cleveland, Ohio.

4. Also known as the Disciples of Christ.

5. Smith, *History of the Church*, vol. 1, pp. 120–25, 146.

6. B. H. Roberts, ed. *A Comprehensive History of the Church of Jesus Christ of Latter-day Saints*, vol. 1, pp. 205–206.

7. Joseph Smith, Jr., "Section LVIII" from *Doctrine and Covenants of the Church of the Latter Day Saints: Carefully Selected from the Revelations of God*, pp. 186–87. The original version of this book is used in this work since subsequent editions have edited and reorganized the original writings of Smith.

8. Throughout the history of the church, Mormons have aggressively proselytized Native Americans. This missionary effort differs from the spiritual colonialism of the time in that Mormon theology teaches that Native Americans are among God's chosen people. This is covered in more detail later in this chapter.

9. Smith, *Doctrine and Covenants*, "Section XXVII," pp. 154–55.

10. The Mormon "Zion" is now a part of Kansas City, Missouri.

11. Gordon B. Hinckley, *Truth Restored: A Short History of the Church of Jesus Christ of Latter-day Saints*, pp. 36, 55. Originally six members were listed on church rolls to fulfill New York State law, although several dozen actually attended.

12. Removal of Native American tribes throughout the nineteenth century was certainly on a larger scale both in brutality and numbers of people affected.

13. For a detailed accounting of reasons for Mormon persecution see Arrington and Bitton, "Early Persecutions," in *The Mormon Experience*, pp. 44–64. See also the anti-Mormon manifesto written in Liberty, Missouri, in 1836: Smith, *History of the Church*, vol. 2, pp. 448–52.

14. Studies of the diverse theological roots of Mormonism can be found in Fawn M. Brodie, *No Man Knows My History: The Life of Joseph Smith, the Mormon Prophet*; D. Michael Quinn, *Early Mormonism and the Magic World View*; and John L. Brooke, *The Refiner's Fire: The Making of Mormon Cosmology, 1644–1844*.

15. Arrington and Bitton, pp. 46–48, 53, and Brodie, p. 233.

16. Arrington and Bitton, pp. 49–50. In the Mormon context a Gentile is any non-Mormon. See Appendix A for more Mormon terminology.

17. Ibid., p. 62. A good example is Nauvoo, Illinois, where the church's holdings were sold cheaply or abandoned. The city's new occupants quickly destroyed all signs of the religion and pretended that the Mormons had never been there. See also Roger D. Launius, *Joseph Smith III: Pragmatic Prophet*, p. 54, which gives a firsthand accounting of post-Mormon Nauvoo.

18. Donna Hill, *Joseph Smith: The First Mormon*, pp. 379–86. Joseph Smith was racially progressive for his time. Although he stopped short of claiming equality, he allowed African Americans into the church and his priesthood. In later years, Brigham Young would codify the racial theories that placed African Americans on a lower spiritual level than all other races. These theories were officially repudiated by the church in 1978, although the vague language of the repudiation has led to some confusion on the exact stand of the contemporary church on this issue. Brodie argues that Smith was not truly committed to abolition and cites his contradictory statements regarding the issue. She does allow for the possibility that Smith's ambiguity toward slavery may have been a function of his trying to avoid further problems in Missouri and Illinois; see Brodie, pp. 173–74, 365.

19. Arrington and Bitton, pp. 48–49. As is the case with the issue of slavery and abolition, some historians believe that Mormons were not as benevolent to Native Americans as they appeared. The author recognizes but does not agree with these interpretations. The purposes of this study is not to argue these points but only to establish that non-Mormon communities perceived Mormons as allies and conspirators with both Native Americans and African Americans.

20. For the revelation regarding the "United Order of Zion" see Smith, "Section XCVIII, paragraph 9," in *Doctrine and Covenants,* pp. 243.

21. Arrington and Bitton, pp. 46–47, 50.

22. Ibid., pp. 54–55. Gov. Thomas Ford of Illinois admitted that such charges were exaggerated. However, there was a group of vigilante Mormons called Danites. This highly secretive group was often implicated in Mormon crimes as its members sought to avenge the loss of life and property suffered by the Mormons. For more information about the operation of the Danites, see D. Michael Quinn, *The Mormon Hierarchy: Origins of Power,* pp.92–103.

23. Donna Hill, pp. 159–60.

24. These demands were based on an earlier manifesto written as a result of the anti-Mormon preachings of Reverend Pixley in Jackson County. See Smith, *History of the Church,* vol. 1, pp. 372–76.

25. Smith, "Expulsion of the Saints of Jackson County," in *History of the Church,* vol. 1, pp. 426–40. The name *Diahmen* is a shortened version of the name *Adam-ondi-Ahman,* which Smith claimed to mean "the valley of god where Adam dwelt" in the language spoken by Adam. It was named by Smith, who said that this was the place where Adam lived after being expelled from the Garden of Eden.

26. Donna Hill, pp. 168–84. See also Paul Bailey, "Zion's Camp," in *The Armies of God: The Little-Known Story of the Mormon Militia on the American Frontier,* pp. 1–29.

27. Donna Hill, pp. 229–34.

28. Smith, *History of the Church,* vol. 3, p. 175.

29. This became known as the Haun's Mill Massacre. Eighteen died as a result of the attack. See Donna Hill, pp. 235–40, and Le Sueur, pp. 162–68.

30. Roger D. Launius. *Alexander William Doniphan: Portrait of a Missouri Moderate,* pp. 60–65.

31. Roberts, vol. 1, pp. 241–55. Although Sheriff William Morgan claimed innocence in letting the Mormons free, he was attacked by a mob and eventually died from his injuries. See Launius, pp. 70–71.

32. Flanders, p. 1.

33. Smith, *History of the Church,* vol. 4, p. 80. Unbeknownst to Smith, the federal government actually lacked jurisdiction in the case.

34. Ibid., pp. 93–94. For Bennett's biography, see Andrew F. Smith, *The Saintly Scoundrel: The Life and Times of Dr. John Cook Bennett.*

35. Smith, *History of the Church,* vol. 4, pp. 58–61.

36. Brodie, p. 458. For an exhaustive study of Joseph Smith's polygamy, see Todd Compton, *In Sacred Loneliness: The Plural Wives of Joseph Smith.*

37. Andrew F. Smith, pp. 80–85.

38. Roberts, *Comprehensive History*, vol. 1, p. 97.

39. Flanders, "The British Mission and Gathering," in *Nauvoo*, pp. 57–91.

40. Joseph Smith, Jr., Nauvoo City Charter, section 25.

41. Bailey, "Nauvoo Legion," in *The Armies of God*, pp. 78–138.

42. Ibid., p. 99.

43. While it is difficult to find consensus on which city was larger, it is clear that Nauvoo and Chicago were close in size in 1844.

44. Roberts, "The Fall of Dr. John C. Bennett," in *Comprehensive History*, vol. 2, pp. 140–46; Andrew F. Smith, pp. 134–36; and Brodie, "The Bennett Explosion," in *No Man Knows*, pp. 309–27.

45. Brodie, p. 318.

46. Smith, *History of the Church*, vol. 5, pp. xvii–xxvi.

CHAPTER 3

1. *Warsaw Signal*, June 12, 1844. "War and extermination is inevitable! CITIZENS ARISE, ONE AND ALL!!! Can you *stand* by, and suffer such INFERNAL DEVILS! to ROB men of their property rights, without avenging them. We have no time for comment! Everyman will make his own. LET IT BE WITH POWDER AND BALL!" Quoted from Flanders, p. 308.

2. He ran as an independent.

3. Smith's journal entry of October 29, 1843, reads "ordained Wm. C. Steffey an Elder who was going to Texas on business." Joseph Smith, Jr., *An American Prophet's Record: The Diaries and Journals of Joseph Smith*, pp. 424–25.

4. *Wasp*, April 16, 1842, and May 14, 1842.

5. For example, compare with Smith's writings about Zion's Camp on June 19, 1834, where he alludes to the "God of Battles" defending the Saints. Smith, *History of the Church*, vol. 2, p. 105.

6. *Wasp*, June 26, 1842.

7. Ibid., September 3, 1842.

8. See Appendix B for a listing of Texas articles in Mormon newspapers in Nauvoo from 1842 through 1845.

9. The editor of the *Wasp* was Smith's brother William. The editor of the *Nauvoo Neighbor* was John Taylor, a member of Smith's Quorum of the Twelve Apostles.

10. For an example of the newspaper's influence on his political views, see Smith, *American Prophet's Record*, p. 456.

11. Marvin S. Hill, *Quest for Refuge: The Mormon Flight from American Pluralism*, pp. 106–109.

12. Quinn, *The Mormon Hierarchy*, p. 120.

13. Smith, *An American Prophet's Record*, p. 456.

14. Smith, *History of the Church*, vol. 6, pp. 334–340. Also Quinn, *The Mormon Hierarchy*, pp. 117–20.

15. Smith, *History of the Church*, vol. 6, pp. 243–44.

16. This policy was similar to the one proposed earlier by Benjamin Lundy. See Campbell, p. 76.

17. Smith, *History of the Church*, vol. 6, pp. 243–44.

18. Ibid.

19. Ibid., p. 270.

20. Ibid., pp. 275–77.

21. Smith, *American Prophet's Record*, p. 462. Smith saw his church as being independent of the United States and therefore appointed ambassadors to the U.S. government, France, England, Russia, Texas, and perhaps other nations. The results of Hyde's diplomatic mission are addressed in the next chapter. This is not to say that Mormon "ambassadors" were recognized as true diplomats by these nations. In the United States they were seen as little more than lobbyists.

22. To read the Hebrew concept of the tribe of Joseph and its promised blessings see Genesis, chapter 49, in the Holy Bible, Authorized King James Version.

23. Joseph Smith, Jr., "Alma, Chapter VII," from the Book of Mormon: An Account Written by the Hand of Mormon, upon Plates Taken from the Plates of Nephi, pp. 246–47. The original version is used here since subsequent editions have corrected the grammar and reorganized the original writings of Smith.

24. Smith, "Section LXV," in *Doctrine and Covenants*, p. 192.

25. There are numerous examples of positive Mormon–Native American relationships during the church's early history. The Mormon association with Native Americans caused enough alarm among other Euro-Americans to be given as a justification for driving the Mormons from Missouri. Smith, *History of the Church*, vol. 2, p. 450.

26. Aztec history itself was reported to correspond with the Book of Mormon. Mormon writers of the time claimed Aztlan to be the Great Lakes region; see the Mormon religious newspaper in Nauvoo, the *Times and Seasons*, "Traits of the Mosaic History Found among the Azteca People," June 15, 1842.

27. Since opposing views were often printed in Nauvoo newspapers, it is not unusual to find differing opinions about the character of Mexicans. Outside of the Texas context, Mexicans faired well in the Nauvoo press.

28. *Times and Seasons*, November 15, 1842.

29. Smith, "An Ordinance in Relation to Religious Societies," in *History of the Church*, vol. 4, p. 306.

30. To read about the origins of anti-Catholic and anti-Spanish feeling in

Europe, see William S. Maltby, *The Black Legend: The Development of Anti-Spanish Sentiment, 1558–1660.*

31. While Díaz often welcomed foreigners into Mexico, it is surprising that he would overlook the Mormon's overt practice of polygamy. For specific details on meetings between Díaz and Mormons and the position of polygamy in Mexico, see B. Carmon Hardy, *Solemn Covenant: The Mormon Polygamous Passage,* pp. 173–76, and Richard S. Van Wagoner, *Mormon Polygamy: A History,* p. 161.

32. James S. Brown, *Life of a Pioneer: Being the Autobiography of James S. Brown,* p. 28.

33. Smith, *History of the Church,* vol. 6, p. 222.

34. *Nauvoo Neighbor,* January 10, 1844.

35. Ibid., January 17, 1844.

36. The Book of Mormon is filled with references to large cities and temples in the Americas. With American archaeology in its infancy, Smith saw every discovery of ruins as proof of the civilizations found in his book. Nauvoo's religious newspaper, the *Times and Seasons,* frequently printed articles about archaeological evidence of the Book of Mormon.

37. Found in Houston and Galveston newspapers.

38. They were reported to have arrived around 1834. Based on this date and their location, the group was most likely the Bastrop Colony; see Don H. Biggers, *German Pioneers in Texas: A Brief History of Their Hardships, Struggles and Achievements,* pp. 8–11.

39. *Nauvoo Neighbor,* February 7, 1844.

40. Lyman Wight was one of the Quorum of the Twelve Apostles that made up the upper power structure directly under Smith.

41. Smith, *History of the Church,* vol. 6, pp. 255–56.

42. Ibid., pp. 257–60.

43. These slaveholders included the Cherokee Nation. While this contradicted Smith's abolitionist views, it is telling that Wight assumed that Smith might consider other alternatives to appeal to potential southern converts.

44. Smith, *American Prophet's Record,* p. 458.

45. "Minutes of the Council of Fifty," April 10, 1880.

46. Smith, *American Prophet's Record,* p. 458.

47. Several important works written on the Council of Fifty include Klaus J. Hansen, *Quest for Empire: The Political Kingdom of God and the Council of Fifty in Mormon History,* and Quinn, *The Mormon Hierarchy.* The group is assumed to have disbanded by the end of the nineteenth century.

48. Hansen, p. 214. An official reply to the author for a request to see the Council of Fifty minutes states merely that the minutes are not available for research: Steven R. Sorensen to Michael Scott Van Wagenen, August 3, 1998.

49. Quinn, *The Mormon Hierarchy,* pp. 120–34.

50. Ibid., pp. 126–28.

51. George Miller, *Correspondence of Bishop George Miller With the Northern Islander. From his first acquaintance with Mormonism up to near the close of his life. Written by himself in the year 1855*, p. 20.

52. *Nauvoo Neighbor*, March 13, 1844.

53. Smith, *History of the Church*, vol. 4, p. 80.

54. Pletcher, p. 135.

55. Smith, *History of the Church*, vol. 6, p. 326.

56. Smith, *An American Prophet's Record*, p. 459.

57. *Nauvoo Neighbor*, March 19, 1844. While reports circulated in the 1840s about dissatisfaction with Mexican rule, Santa Fe remained in control of Mexico until the U.S.–Mexican War. See Weems, p. 197.

CHAPTER 4

1. See Houston's instructions to Isaac Van Zandt in Sam Houston, *The Writings of Sam Houston, 1813–1863*, vol. 3, pp. 538–41.

2. Pletcher, pp. 135–38.

3. Houston, *Autobiography*, p. 203.

4. Ibid., pp. 202–203.

5. Smith, *An American Prophet's Record*, p. 476. Smith records the date of the report as May 3, 1844.

6. Miller, pp. 20–21.

7. Houston, *Autobiography*, pp. 204–206.

8. *Journal History of the Church*, April 2, 1847. The *Journal History of the Church* is a large, multivolume record of the daily occurrences in the Church of Jesus Christ of Latter-day Saints, from its beginnings in 1830 to today. The only public copy is kept in the Church Historical Office in Salt Lake City.

9. Quoted in Richard E. Bennett, *Mormons at the Missouri, 1846–1852: "And Should We Die . . . ,"* p. 158.

10. El Fronton de Santa Isabel was also called Point Isabel, now known as Port Isabel in Cameron County, Texas. Isla Brazos de Santiago is now called Brazos Island, also in Cameron County.

11. Miller, p. 21. Miller's account actually lists "A. W. Brown," but there was no such person on the Council of Fifty, see Hansen, p. 233. On February 22, 1999, the author had a phone conversation with D. Michael Quinn to discuss this discrepancy. Quinn makes a thorough study of the Mormon ambassador phenomena in *The Mormon Hierarchy*. He believes that the *Northern Islander* misprinted the name. It should actually read "A. W. Babbitt." Almon W. Babbitt was a member of the Council of Fifty who was deeply involved in Mormon politics at the time.

12. He once wrote "I am the biggest advocate of the Constitution of the

United States there is on the earth." See Smith, *An American Prophet's Record*, p. 420; see also pp. 160–61, 312–13.

13. Smith expounds on these views in a critical letter written to Democratic presidential candidate Sen. John C. Calhoun, on January 2, 1844. His description of politicians manipulating the Constitution is similar to his earlier descriptions of ministers manipulating the Bible. See Smith, *History of the Church*, vol. 6, pp. 156–62, and compare to vol. 1, pp. 2–4.

14. Miller, p. 21.

15. There are several good works addressing the life of Lyman Wight. Two important biographies are Philip C. Wightman, "The Life and Contributions of Lyman Wight," and Jermy Benton Wight, *The Wild Ram of the Mountain: The Story of Lyman Wight.*

16. Many tribes differentiated between Mormons and other Euro-Americans. The common terminology used in the Rocky Mountains for example was *Mericats* for Americans and *Mormonee* for Mormons. See "Mormons and Native Americans," in Arrington and Bitton, pp. 145–60.

17. Miller, p. 18.

18. Smith, *History of the Church*, vol. 6, pp. 255–56.

19. Miller, p. 19. Here Miller discusses saving the life of a Northern Chippewa chief who had been severely beaten by Euro-American traders. He further provided provisions for the tribe and told the chief that "the United States was no friend of ours; that they had robbed us, and permitted us to be plundered by the white man; and further, if we let them have food it would not be for the love we had for the United States, but for that we had toward the abused and oppressed Indians."

20. In 1845, when Wight did relocate the company to central Texas, the Mormons were known and sought after for their milling skills.

21. Smith, *An American Prophet's Record*, pp. 476–77. These ambassadors were not sent for proselyting purposes; rather they handled themselves as diplomats representing a legitimate nation.

22. Quinn, *The Mormon Hierarchy*, pp. 132–34.

23. As quoted in Hyrum L. Andrus, *Joseph Smith and World Government*, p. 53. This source cites the origin of this article to be a later typescript of the Lee County (Iowa) *Democrat*, vol. 3, no. 27, dated incorrectly as January 20, 1844. Some of the information is accurate, including the fact that both Mexican generals operated near the Texas border and that Miller was chosen as a Mormon commissioner to Texas. Who "tigertail" was is unclear. William W. Phelps, a member of the Mormon hierarchy, called the Twelve Apostles by cryptic animal nicknames: e.g., Lyman Wight was the Wild Ram of the Mountain, Brigham

Young the Lion of the Lord. Perhaps "tigertail" is making mocking reference to Young.

24. During the Republic Period, Texans launched retaliatory raids in northern Mexico and were defeated at Mier by Mexican forces under General Ampudia. President Lamar also fostered plans for a Texas assault on the Mexican city of Matamoros. Both Mier and Matamoros would border the Mormon Kingdom of God and benefit from the security of the buffer state.

25. See Smith's journal for the two-month period from April 26, 1844, to June 22, 1844, in Smith, *An American Prophet's Record*, pp. 472–96.

26. *Journal History*, April 30, 1844.

27. Ibid., June 1, 1844.

28. Smith, *History of the Church*, vol. 6, p. 372.

29. Ibid., p. 373.

30. Ibid., p. 375. This was the map made by the John C. Fremont Expedition. Douglas may have been encouraging the Mormon migration to help resolve the growing Mormon-Gentile conflict in Illinois. A one-time friend of Smith's, Douglas turned against the Mormons during the Utah War of 1857–58. In a move that seemed by Mormons to be motivated by political advantage, Douglas encouraged the military occupation of Utah although he was clearly in a position to help stop it. See Smith, *History of the Church*, vol. 5, pp. 393–98, especially regarding Smith's prophecy about Douglas's political career.

31. *Journal History*, April 30, 1844.

32. Quinn, *The Mormon Hierarchy*, p. 120.

33. *Journal History*, April 30, 1844.

34. Smith, *History of the Church*, vol. 6, p. 370n.

35. *Journal History*, April 30, 1844.

36. A popular song written in Nauvoo by Apostle John Taylor, "The Upper California," includes the following lyrics: "The Saints can be supported there, and taste the sweets of liberty / In Upper California, Oh, that's the land for me! ... We'll burst off all our fetters, and break the Gentile yoke / For long it has beset us, but now it shall be broke / No more shall Jacob bow the neck / Henceforth he shall be great and free / in Upper California, Oh, that's the land for me." see CD liner notes, *Nauvoo Brass Bands*.

37. *Journal History*, April 30, 1844.

38. *Nauvoo Neighbor*, June 12, 1844.

39. Ibid., June 5, 12, 19, and 26, 1844.

40. Smith, *History of the Church*, vol. 6, p. 507. Little is known about this man except for a few short references made in Smith's records. Smith had a loyal Gentile friend and lawyer by the same surname, so perhaps there was some relationship.

41. Ibid., p. 554.

42. Because of the letter's close proximity to Smith's murder, whether he ever read the letter is unknown.

43. John H. Walton to Joseph Smith, June 3, 1844. This land is north of modern-day Dallas. The amount of land is described as "60 leagues," which is a linear measurement of 180 miles. Perhaps Walton was selling 180 square miles, roughly the size of a small Texas county.

44. This is where the U.S.–Mexican War began in 1846.

45. There is evidence that perhaps Young knew of Smith's change of plans when he said, "Let the U.S. give us the north part of Texas, let us go where we please." Without further detail it is impossible to determine if he was referring to the Southwick and Walton proposals or if he meant the northwestern reaches of the Republic, which at the time stretched into the Rocky Mountains. Quinn, *Mormon Hierarchy*, p. 200.

46. Roberts, vol. 2, pp. 227–39.

47. Smith, *History of the Church*, vol. 6, pp. 605–606.

48. Smith, *An American Prophet's Record*, p. 495.

49. Roberts, vol. 2, pp. 246–48.

50. Ibid., p. 249.

51. Smith, *History of the Church*, vol. 6, p. 554.

52. Ibid., pp. 556–57.

53. Taylor would eventually become the third president of the church after Young's death in 1877.

54. The authoritative source on Smith's assassination is Dallin H. Oaks and Marvin S. Hill, *The Carthage Conspiracy: The Trial of the Accused Assassins of Joseph Smith*.

CHAPTER 5

1. Smith had two counselors, Sidney Rigdon and William Law, who, with him, comprised what is called the First Presidency.

2. D. Michael Quinn, "The Mormon Succession Crisis of 1844," *Brigham Young University Studies* 16 (Winter, 1976), pp. 187–233.

3. Lucien Woodworth to Sam Houston, July 11, 1844.

4. Roberts, vol. 2, pp. 416–20.

5. Miller, p. 24.

6. *Journal History*, April 2, 1847.

7. Ibid., May 3, 1844.

8. Woodworth to Houston, July 11, 1844. Woodworth wrote to Houston in regard to Smith's murderers: "some I am informed have already started for Texas."

9. Smith, *History of the Church*, vol. 6, p. 222.

10. Lyman Wight, *An Address by Way of an Abridged Account and Journal of my life from February 1844 Up to April 1848, With an Appeal to the Latter-day Saints*, pp. 3–4.

11. Ibid., p. 6. For details regarding the long-running rivalry and power struggle between Wight and Young, see Davis Bitton, "The Ram and the Lion: Lyman Wight and Brigham Young."

12. Smith, *History of the Church*, vol. 7, pp. 248–49. Entries made after Smith's death were compiled by scribes and editors.

13. Ibid., pp. 254–55.

14. Wightman, pp. 93–96. Although Wightman does not draw the conclusion that the power struggle drove Wight from the city, it is a safe assumption based on the bad feeling that existed between Young and Wight from that time forward.

15. The first threats of excommunication did not occur until 1848. See Wightman, pp. 105–108.

16. George Miller was particularly critical of Wight's bad business habits. See Miller, pp. 23, 41, 42.

17. There are several fanciful versions of this dramatic departure in Wisconsin folklore. See Albert H. Sanford, "The Mormons of Coulee Ridge," *Wisconsin Magazine of History* 24 (December, 1940), and Dennis Rowley, "The Mormon Experience in the Wisconsin Pineries, 1841–1845," *Brigham Young University Studies* 32, nos. 1–2 (1992).

18. Lyman Wight, *An Address*, p. 8. Here Wight described his five weeks in Iowa without giving an explanation for his not visiting Nauvoo.

19. Wight kept a journal of his travels; however, this valuable document was burned in a fire in 1907. Prior to that time, his great-grandson Heman Hale Smith (also a great-grandson of Joseph Smith, Jr.) wrote Wight's history using the journal. Many specifics mentioned in this chapter come from Smith's work and are the closest source to Wight's original journal. See Heman Hale Smith, "The Lyman Wight Colony in Texas."

20. Smith, *History of the Church*, vol. 5, p. 85.

21. Wight was an early convert of Sidney Rigdon's Campbellite community. He was one of the hundreds of Campbellites from that town to join the Mormon faith in 1830. See Wightman, p. 14.

22. An oft-quoted scripture from Mormon theology can be found in Smith, *The Book of Mormon*, pp. 9–10, which reads, "I will go and do the things which the Lord hath commanded, for I know that the Lord giveth no commandments unto the children of men, save he shall prepare a way for them that they may accomplish the thing which he commandeth them." This remains to this day a source of great optimism and motivation for Mormons.

23. Quinn, "The Mormon Succession Crisis of 1844," pp. 223–24.

24. Joseph Smith III remained indifferent to his religion until 1860, when he finally stepped forward to assume the role of the president of the Reorganized Church of Jesus Christ of Latter Day Saints—a smaller branch of the church that refused to follow Young to Utah. See Quinn, "The Mormon Succession Crisis of 1844," pp. 222–32, and also the Launius biography of Joseph Smith III.

25. Two important works on Wight's colonization of Texas include unpublished manuscripts by Davis Bitton, "Mormons in Texas: The Ill-Fated Lyman Wight Colony," and T. R. Turk, "Mormons in Texas: The Lyman Wight Colony."

26. Wight, *An Address*, p. 8, and also C. Stanley Banks, "The Mormon Migration into Texas," *Southwestern Historical Quarterly* 49 (July–April, 1946).

27. H. H. Smith, p. 11.

28. Much of the work on the act itself was done under the Tyler administration. See Sam W. Haynes, *James K. Polk and the Expansionist Impulse*, p. 54.

29. Mark E. Nackham, *A Nation within a Nation: The Rise of Texas Nationalism*, pp. 105–109.

30. For a list of all demands put on the Mormons, see Leonard J. Arrington, *Brigham Young: American Moses*, p. 125.

31. Ibid., p. 127.

32. Ibid., pp. 124–29.

33. H. H. Smith, p. 12.

34. See again the description of the original proposed Kingdom of God in Miller, p. 20.

35. Noah Smithwick, *The Evolution of a State: Recollections of Old Texas Days*, pp. 235–36.

36. H. H. Smith, p. 12.

37. Wight was a colonel in the Nauvoo Legion—a title he retained, at least honorarily, throughout the rest of his life. This description was originally given by a Methodist minister in Austin, quoted in Wightman, p. 100.

38. Smithwick, pp. 235–36. The "objectional features" no doubt included polygamy, which was practiced by at least three men in the community, including Wight himself; see Wightman, p. 103.

39. J. B. Wight, pp. 276–80.

40. Ibid., p. 328. J. B. Wight's genealogical research shows the addition of at least one German to Wight's group during the Fredericksburg years. She came to Zodiac after marrying a Mormon and presumably joining the faith.

41. Ibid., pp. 278–80, 283–85.

42. Arrington and Bitton, pp. 100–101. Popular folklore has Young saying simply, "This is the place!"

43. The authoritative biography of Emma Smith is Linda King Newell and Valeen Tippetts Avery, *Mormon Enigma: Emma Hale Smith*.

44. J. B. Wight, pp. 433–34.

45. Miller, pp. 36–38.

46. Ibid., p. 41.

47. Ibid.

48. Although Mormons have had a health code against the use of tobacco and alcohol since 1833, it was initially only a suggestion and not a required standard of living until the late 1800s. Heavy drinking, however, was seen as a sign of personal weakness and frowned upon. See Smith, "Section LXXX," *Doctrine and Covenants*, pp. 207–208.

49. Several contemporary writers discuss Wight's alcoholism. George Miller, ever unsympathetic, makes the point bluntly, in Miller, p. 42. Wight's son makes mention of his father's opium addiction in his memoirs; see Levi Lamoni Wight, *The Reminiscences and Civil War Letters of Levi Lamoni Wight: Life in a Mormon Colony on the Texas Frontier*, p. 19.

50. J. B. Wight, p. 310.

51. This growth can be explained through converts, births, and other Mormons from the north joining the community. The population statistics are explained in great detail in the "Demography" chapter of J. B. Wight, pp. 322–43.

52. Deseret was Young's version of the Kingdom of God. Geographically it covered all or parts of the modern states of Utah, Idaho, Nevada, Arizona, California, Oregon, Wyoming, Colorado, and New Mexico. While it existed de facto from 1847 until 1858, its official declared existence was from 1849 to 1851. After the land fell into American hands, Young applied for statehood and was denied. The federal government organized the Utah Territory from the central land of Deseret and appointed Young as the first governor. The name *Deseret* comes from a word in the Book of Mormon said to mean "honeybee." This no doubt refers to the Mormon United Order, which was symbolized by a beehive. Thus Utah is known as the Beehive State.

53. Smith, *History of the Church*, vol. 7, pp. 301–302.

54. The full accounting of the elders can be found in the unpublished journal of Preston Thomas, a manuscript of which is in the LDS Church Historical Office.

55. Wightman, pp. 109–10. Disfellowshipping in the Mormon religion was not as severe as excommunication. It generally meant that the individual lost all position in the church while maintaining his or her basic rights of membership. Wight would have lost his calling as an apostle as a result.

56. The first missionaries to Texas under Brigham Young were Preston Thomas and Amasa Lyman, see Thomas, p. 42.

57. Ibid., p. 38.

58. Melvin C. Johnson, "Lone Star Trails to Zion: Mormon Narratives of the Republic and State of Texas, 1844–1858," p. 5. This is the manuscript for a presentation by the same name at the Sunstone Symposium in Salt Lake City in August, 1998. It is the basis for an upcoming book to be called "Mormon Voices from the Texas Dust," which is part of the Arthur H. Clark Company's Kingdom in the West: The Mormons and the American Frontier series.

59. Lyman Wight to Brigham Young, March 2, 1857.

60. Wightman, p. 111.

61. Now called Mormon Mill. It is near present-day Marble Falls, Burnet County, Texas.

62. J. B. Wight, p. 361.

63. Ibid., p. 364.

64. Ibid., p. 374.

65. Smithwick, p. 225.

66. Ibid., p. 229. These families eventually immigrated to California.

67. J. B. Wight, pp. 382–87.

68. Ibid., p. 388.

69. Ibid., p. 392.

70. Robert S. Neighbors, Indian agent, to Lyman Wight and others, March 26, 1855; quoted in J. B. Wight, pp. 398–99.

71. On March 7, 1856, Wight wrote an impassioned letter to Texas governor Elisha M. Pease asking for financial assistance because of the great losses at the hands of the Comanches. See H. H. Smith, pp. 46–47.

72. Lyman Wight to Benjamin Wight, April 4, 1856. Two examples of these Mormon chairs are known to exist: one in a museum in Bandera, Texas, and the other in possession of the author.

73. H. H. Smith, p. 51. On December 25, 1832, Joseph Smith also had prophesied of the coming of a civil war that would begin in South Carolina. This revelation can be found in its entirety in Smith et al., Section 87 of the modern LDS *Doctrine and Covenants.*

74. L. L. Wight, *Reminiscences,* p. 25. Abolitionists suffered great persecution in Texas during the Civil War. It is likely that the Mormons too might have faired poorly during this time. After the breakup of the settlement, several young men, including three of Wight's sons, fought for the Confederacy.

75. J. B. Wight, p. 422.

76. Ibid., p. 423.

77. J. B. Wight makes this assumption based on his research; see p. 423–24.

Laudanum refers to any number of old common medications that used opium as their main active ingredient.

78. A Mormon cemetery can still be found in the ruins of the town, just outside of Fredericksburg. Wight's grave has not yet been identified.

79. A good follow-up on the lives of the Texas Mormons can be found in J. B. Wight, pp. 334–40.

CHAPTER 6

1. Paul Horgan, *Great River: The Rio Grande in North American History*, pp. 603–604.

2. T. R. Fehrenbach, *Lone Star: A History of Texas and the Texans*, pp. 268–70.

3. Ibid., pp. 270–71.

4. In modern-day Brownsville, in Cameron County, Texas.

5. Horgan, pp. 609–12, 660–95.

6. Bailey, pp. 192–94. These territorial appointments were typically made as repayment of political favors rather than being based on merit. Sen. Sam Houston publicly questioned the character of the Utah appointees in Congress. See Houston, *Writings of Sam Houston*, vol. 6, pp. 492–93.

7. Arrington and Bitton, p. 165. The Mormons particularly loathed Drummond, who openly associated with a prostitute and was considered a liar.

8. Ibid., pp. 164–68. Although these accusations were not initially true, the approach of the army necessitated such alliances. In August, 1857, a combined force of Mormons and Native Americans massacred a Missouri immigrant train whose members had poisoned several Native Americans and were thought to be an advance party of the U.S. invasion force. The best source on this tragic event is Juanita Brooks, *The Mountain Meadows Massacre*.

9. Arrington and Bitton, pp. 164–69.

10. George A. Crosby, "A Crosby Memoir Letter." The original is in the LDS Church Historian's Office, Salt Lake City, Utah. Some details are confused because the letter is the recounting of story as passed through several people and generations. The blanket is obviously Houston's famous Cherokee cloak. Utah Mormons might easily have mistaken this for the colorful Navajo blankets with which they themselves were acquainted.

11. The Mormons bought these outposts in 1855; see Arrington and Bitton, p. 118.

12. Ibid., pp. 166–67.

13. Houston's speeches to Congress in regard to the Utah War can be found in their entirety in Houston, *Writings of Sam Houston*, vol. 6, pp. 466–529.

14. Ibid., p. 504.

15. Ibid. Throughout his speeches regarding this issue, he makes several jests. The Congressional Record even makes note of the laughter.

16. Ibid., p. 507.

17. Ibid., p. 525.

18. Arrington, *Brigham Young*, pp. 264–67.

19. For details related to the Mormon military operations in the Utah War, see Arrington, *Brigham Young*, pp. 250–71, and Bailey, pp. 185–256.

20. Houston, *Writings of Sam Houston*, vol. 6, pp. 524–25.

21. Ibid., pp. 525–27.

22. Arrington and Bitton, pp. 166–69.

23. Bailey, pp. 247–53.

24. Approximately two hundred thousand Mormons live in Texas, per the *Houston Chronicle*, February 10, 1997, and allowing for typical growth patterns between 1997 and 1999. The RLDS Church has also grown in Texas over the years and has several thousand members in the state. Today there are perhaps hundreds of sects that follow the teachings of Joseph Smith, Jr. Because some of these groups continue to practice polygamy, it is difficult to find exact statistics. See Steven L. Shields, *Divergent Paths of the Restoration: A History of the Latter-day Saint Movement*.

Bibliography

PRIMARY SOURCES

Brown, James S. *Life of a Pioneer: Being the Autobiography of James S. Brown.* Salt Lake City: Geo. Q. Cannon & Sons, 1900.

Crosby, George A. "Crosby Memoir Letter." LDS Church Historian's Office, Salt Lake City, Utah, October 15, 1929.

Graebner, Norman A., ed. *Manifest Destiny.* New York: Bobbs-Merrill, 1968.

The Holy Bible. Authorized King James Version. Salt Lake City: The Church of Jesus Christ of Latter-day Saints, 1979.

Houston, Sam. *The Autobiography of Sam Houston.* Edited by Donald Day and Harry H. Ullom. Norman: University of Oklahoma Press, 1954.

————. *The Writings of Sam Houston, 1813–1863.* 6 volumes. Edited by Amelia W. Williams and Eugene C. Barker. Austin: University of Texas Press, 1941.

Journal History of the Church of Jesus Christ of Latter-day Saints, 1830–2001. A multivolume, daily record of the Church of Jesus Christ of Latter-day Saints. LDS Church Historian's Office, Salt Lake City, Utah.

Miller, George. *Correspondence of Bishop George Miller With the Northern Islander. From his first acquaintance with Mormonism up to near the close of his life. Written by himself in the year 1855.* Burlington, Wis.: Wingfield Watson, 1916.

"Minutes of the Council of Fifty." Unpublished manuscript, Brigham Young University Special Collections, Provo, Utah, April 10, 1880.

Roberts, B. H., ed. *A Comprehensive History of the Church of Jesus Christ of Latter-day Saints.* Reprint Edition. 6 Volumes. Provo, Utah: Brigham Young University Press, 1965.

Smith, Joseph, Jr. *An American Prophet's Record: The Diaries and Journals of Joseph Smith.* Edited by Scott H. Faulring. Salt Lake City: Signature Books, 1989.

————. The Book of Mormon: An Account Written by the Hand of

Mormon, upon Plates Taken from the Plates of Nephi. 1830. Reprint, Independence, Mo.: Herald House, 1970.

————. *Doctrine and Covenants of the Church of Jesus Christ of the Latter Day Saints: Carefully Selected from the Revelations of God.* 1835. Reprint, Independence, Mo.: Herald House, 1971.

———— et al. *The Doctrine and Covenants of the Church of Latter-day Saints: Containing Revelations Given to Joseph Smith, the Prophet, with Some Additions by His Successors in the Presidency of the Church.* Salt Lake City: The Church of Jesus Christ of Latter-day Saints, 1981.

————. *History of the Church of Jesus Christ of Latter-day Saints.* Edited by B. H. Roberts. Second revised edition. 7 volumes. Salt Lake City: Deseret Book Company, 1976.

————. Nauvoo City Charter. LDS Church Historian's Office, Salt Lake City, Utah, 1840.

Smithwick, Noah. *The Evolution of a State: Recollections of Old Texas Days.* Austin, 1900. Most likely self-published.

Sorensen, Steven R., to Michael Van Wagenen, August 3, 1998. In possession of the author, Port Isabel, Tex..

Taylor, John. "The Upper California." *Nauvoo Brass Bands.* Salt Lake City: Covenant Recordings, 1997.

Thomas, Preston. "Preston Thomas: His Life and Travels." Edited by Daniel Thomas. Unpublished manuscript in the LDS Church Historian's Office, 1942.

Walton, John H., to Joseph Smith, June 3, 1844. LDS Church Historian's Office, Salt Lake City, Utah.

Wight, Levi Lamoni. *The Reminiscences and Civil War Letters of Levi Lamoni Wight: Life in a Mormon Colony on the Texas Frontier.* Edited by Davis Bitton. Salt Lake City: University of Utah Press, 1970.

Wight, Lyman. *An Address by Way of an Abridged Account and Journal of my life from February 1844 Up to April 1848, With an Appeal to the Latter-day Saints.* Austin, 1848. Self- published.

———— to Brigham Young, March 2, 1857. LDS Church Historian's Office, Salt Lake City, Utah.

———— to Benjamin Wight, April 4, 1856. Archives of the RLDS Church, Independence, Mo..

Woodworth, Lucien, to Sam Houston, July 11, 1844. LDS Church Historian's Office, Salt Lake City, Utah.

NEWSPAPERS

Lee County (Iowa) *Democrat*
Galveston News

Houston Telegraph
Houston Chronicle
Nauvoo (Illinois) *Neighbor*
Times and Seasons (Nauvoo, Illinois)
Wasp (Nauvoo, Illinois)

SECONDARY SOURCES

Andrus, Hyrum L. *Joseph Smith and World Government.* Salt Lake City: Deseret Book Company, 1963.

Arrington, Leonard J. *Brigham Young: American Moses.* Urbana: University of Illinois Press, 1985.

―――, and Davis Bitton. *The Mormon Experience: The History of the Latter-day Saints.* New York: Alfred A. Knopf, 1979.

Bailey, Paul. *The Armies of God: The Little-Known Story of the Mormon Militia on the American Frontier.* Garden City, N.Y.: Doubleday, 1968.

Banks, Stanley C., "The Mormon Migration into Texas," *Southwestern Historical Quarterly* 49 (July, 1945–April, 1946). Austin: Texas State Historical Association, 1946.

Bennett, Richard E. *Mormons at the Missouri, 1846–1852: "And Should We Die . . . "* Norman: University of Oklahoma Press, 1987.

Biesele, Rudolph Leopold. *The History of the German Settlements in Texas, 1831–1861.* Austin: Press of Von Boeckmann-Jones Co., 1930.

Biggers, Don H. *German Pioneers in Texas: A Brief History of Their Hardships, Struggles and Achievements.* Fredericksburg, Tex.: Press of the Fredericksburg Publishing Co., 1925.

Binkley, William Campbell. *The Expansionist Movement in Texas, 1836–1850.* Berkeley: University of California Press, 1925.

Bitton, Davis. "Mormons in Texas: The Ill-Fated Lyman Wight Colony." Unpublished manuscript. LDS Church Historian's Office, Salt Lake City, Utah, 1968.

―――. "The Ram and the Lion: Lyman Wight and Brigham Young." Unpublished manuscript, LDS Church Historian's Office, Salt Lake City, 1997.

Brack, Gene M. *Mexico Views Manifest Destiny, 1821–1846: An Essay on the Origins of the Mexican War.* Albuquerque: University of New Mexico Press, 1975.

Brice, Donaly E. *The Great Comanche Raid: Boldest Indian Attack on the Texas Republic.* Austin: Eakin Press, 1987.

Brodie, Fawn M. *No Man Knows My History: The Life of Joseph Smith, the Mormon Prophet.* Second edition. New York: Alfred A. Knopf, 1982.

Brooke, John L. *The Refiner's Fire: The Making of Mormon Cosmology, 1644–1844.* Cambridge: Cambridge University Press, 1994.

Brooks, Juanita. *The Mountain Meadows Massacre.* Stanford: Stanford University Press, 1950.

Campbell, Randolph P. *Sam Houston and the American Southwest.* Library of American Biography. Edited by Oscar Handlin. New York: HarperCollins, 1993.

Compton, Todd. *In Sacred Loneliness: The Plural Wives of Joseph Smith.* Salt Lake City: Signature Books, 1997.

Conner, Seymour V. *The Peters Colony of Texas.* Austin: Texas State Historical Association, 1959.

De Bruhl, Marshall. *Sword of San Jacinto: A Life of Sam Houston.* New York: Random House, 1993.

Fehrenbach, T. R. *Lone Star: A History of Texas and the Texans.* New York: American Legacy Press, 1983.

Flanahan, Sue. *Sam Houston's Texas.* Austin: University of Texas Press, 1964.

Flanders, Robert Bruce. *Nauvoo: Kingdom on the Mississippi.* Urbana: University of Illinois Press, 1965.

Friend, Llerena B. *Sam Houston: The Great Designer.* Austin: University of Texas Press, 1954.

Hansen, Klaus J. *Quest for Empire: The Political Kingdom of God and the Council of Fifty in Mormon History.* Lincoln: University of Nebraska Press, 1974.

Hardy, B. Carmon. *Solemn Covenant: The Mormon Polygamous Passage.* Urbana: University of Illinois Press, 1992.

Haynes, Sam W. *James K. Polk and the Expansionist Impulse.* Edited by Oscar Handlin. New York: Addison-Wesley, 1997.

Hill, Donna. *Joseph Smith: The First Mormon.* Reprint edition. Salt Lake City: Signature Books, 1999.

Hill, Marvin S. *Quest for Refuge: The Mormon Flight from American Pluralism.* Salt Lake City: Signature Books, 1989.

Hinckley, Gordon B. *Truth Restored: A Short History of the Church of Jesus Christ of Latter-day Saints.* Revised edition. Salt Lake City: Church of Jesus Christ of Latter-day Saints, 1979.

Horgan, Paul. *Great River: The Rio Grande in North American History.* New York: Holt, Rinehart and Winston, 1954.

James, Marquis. *The Raven: A Biography of Sam Houston.* New York: Blue Ribbon Books, 1929.

Johannsen, Robert W., et al. *Manifest Destiny and Empire: American Antebellum Expansion.* Edited by Sam W. Haynes and Christopher Morris. College Station: Texas A&M University Press, 1997.

Johnson, Melvin C. "Lone Star Trails to Zion: Mormon Narratives of the Republic and State of Texas, 1844–1858." Unpublished manuscript in possession of the author, 1998.

Lamego, General Manuel A. Sanchez. *The Second Mexican-Texan War, 1841–1843.* Translated by J. Hefter. A Hill Junior College Monograph, No. 7. Hillsboro, Tex.: Hill Junior College Press, 1972.

Launius, Roger D. *Alexander William Doniphan: Portrait of a Missouri Moderate.* Columbia: University of Missouri Press, 1997.

————. *Joseph Smith III: Pragmatic Prophet.* Urbana: University of Illinois Press, 1988.

LeSueur, Stephen C. *The 1838 Mormon War in Missouri.* Columbia: University of Missouri Press, 1987.

Lindheim, Milton. *The Republic of the Rio Grande: Texans in Mexico, 1839–1840.* Waco: W. M. Morrison, 1964.

Maltby, William S. *The Black Legend: The Development of Anti-Spanish Sentiment, 1558–1660.* Durham, N. C.: Duke University Press, 1971.

Marvin, Hunter J. "Elder Lyman Wight Brings His Colony to Bandera." In *100 Years in Bandera, 1853–1953.* Bandera, Tex.: Bandera Bulletin, 1953.

Meier, Matt S., and Feliciano Rivera. *Dictionary of Mexican-American History.* Westport, Conn.: Greenwood Press, 1981.

Merk, Frederick. *Manifest Destiny and Mission in American History: A Reinterpretation.* New York: Alfred A. Knopf, 1963.

Nackham, Mark E. *A Nation within a Nation: The Rise of Texas Nationalism.* Port Washington, N.Y.: National University Publications, 1975.

Nance, Joseph Milton. *After San Jacinto: The Texas-Mexican Frontier, 1836–1841.* Austin: University of Texas Press, 1963.

————. *Attack and Counterattack: The Texas-Mexican Frontier, 1842.* Austin: University of Texas Press, 1964.

Nauvoo Brass Bands. Compact disc recording. Salt Lake City, Utah: Covenant Recordings, 1997.

Newell, Linda King, and Valeen Tippetts Avery. *Mormon Enigma: Emma Hale Smith.* Urbana: University of Illinois Press, 1994.

Oaks, Dallin H., and Marvin S. Hill. *The Carthage Conspiracy: The Trial of the Accused Assassins of Joseph Smith.* Urbana: University of Illinois Press, 1979.

O'Neill, Patrick L. "The German Settling of Fisher and Miller Colony in West Central Texas." Unpublished Master's Thesis, West Texas A&M Univeristy, Canyon, Tex., 1997.

Pahissa, Ángela Moyano. *México y Estados Unidos: Orígines de una relación, 1819–1861.* Mexico D. F.: Secretaría de Educación Pública, 1985.

Pierce, Gerald S. *Texas Under Arms: The Camps, Posts, Forts, and Military Towns of the Republic of Texas, 1836–1846.* Austin: Encino Press, 1969.

Pletcher, David M. *The Diplomacy of Annexation: Texas, Oregon, and the Mexican War.* Columbia, Mo.: University of Missouri Press, 1973.

Quinn, D. Michael. *Early Mormonism and the Magic World View.* Revised and enlarged edition. Salt Lake City: Signature Books, 1998.

———. *The Mormon Hierarchy: Origins of Power.* Salt Lake City: Signature Books, 1994.

———. "The Mormon Succession Crisis of 1844." *Brigham Young University Studies* 16 (Winter, 1976): 187–233. Provo: Brigham Young University Press, 1976.

Rowley, Dennis. "The Mormon Experience in the Wisconsin Pineries, 1841–1845." *Brigham Young University Studies* 32, nos. 1–2 (1992): 119–48. Provo: Brigham Young University Press, 1992.

Sanford, Albert H. "The Mormons of Coulee Ridge." *Wisconsin Magazine of History* 24 (December, 1940): 129–42.

Shields, Steven L. *Divergent Paths of the Restoration: A History of the Latter-day Saint Movement.* Bountiful, Utah: Restoration Research, 1982.

Smith, Andrew F. *The Saintly Scoundrel: The Life and Times of Dr. John Cook Bennett.* Urbana: University of Illinois Press, 1997.

Smith, Heman Hale. "The Lyman Wight Colony in Texas." Unpublished manuscript, Brigham Young University Special Collections, Provo, Utah, ca. 1900.

Turk, T. R. *Mormons in Texas: The Lyman Wight Colony.* Unpublished manuscript. Brigham Young University Special Collections, Provo, Utah, 1987.

Totorow, Norman E., *Texas Annexation and the Mexican War: A Political Study of the Old Northwest.* Palo Alto, Calif.: Chadwick House, 1978.

Van Wagoner, Richard S. *Mormon Polygamy: A History.* Salt Lake City: Signature Books, 1986.

Weaver, Bobby. *Castro's Colony: Empresario Development in Texas, 1842–1865.* College Station: Texas A&M University Press, 1985.

Weems, John Edward. *Dream of Empire: A Human History of the Republic of Texas, 1836–1846.* New York: Simon and Schuster, 1971.

Wight, Jermy Benton. *The Wild Ram of the Mountain: The Story of Lyman Wight.* Afton, Wyo.: Afton Thrifty Print, 1996.

Wightman, Philip C. "The Life and Contributions of Lyman Wight." Unpublished master's thesis, Brigham Young University, Provo, Utah, 1971.

Williams, John Hoyt. *Sam Houston: A Biography of the Father of Texas.* New York: Simon & Schuster, 1993.

Index

African Americans: converts to
Mormonism, 16; emancipation, 15,
26; federal slavery issue, 8–9, 65,
71; military alliance with
Mormons, 15, 44; Mormon atti-
tudes, 26, 90n. 18; slaves to the
Cherokee and Choctaw, 32
Alma, 27–28
American Revolution, 5
Ampudia, Pedro de, 41
anti-Mormons, 22–23, 44, 49. *See also*
Latter-day Saints, Church of Jesus
Christ of, persecution of
Argentina, 5
Arkansas, 32
Austin, Texas, 30, 38, 57–58, 60, 72
Aztec People, 93n. 26. *See also*
Lamanites
Aztlan, 93n. 26

Babbitt, Almon W., 40, 44, 53–54,
95n. 95
Bandera, Texas, 61–62,
Bennett, John C., 19–22
Black River Lumber Company, 32–33,
42, 54–55, 59
Boggs, Lilburn, 7, 18, 22

Bolivia, 5
Book of Mormon, 13, 14, 27, 30, 32
Brazil, 5, 32
Buchanan, James, 65, 67, 68, 73
Buchanan's Blunder. *See* Utah War

Calhoun, John C., 19, 96n. 13
California, 29, 30, 42, 46, 55–56, 60,
68, 72, 97n. 36
California, Republic of, 5
Campbell, Alexander, 13
Campbellites, 13–14, 56, 60
Canada, 26
Carthage, Illinois, 21, 50–51
Castroville, Texas, 9
Catholicism, 7, 24–25, 28–29
Cherokee People, 7, 32, 48
Chicago, Illinois, 21
Chihuahua, Mexico, 29
Chile, 5
Choctaw People, 32
Church of Christ, 13. *See also* Latter-day
Saints, Church of Jesus Christ of
Colorado River, 30, 32, 58
Columbia, 5
Comanche People, 9, 39, 58, 62, 71,
102n. 71